The
Good Dad

Praise f... ...Dad

The Good Dad takes an honest look at the common struggles and pressures fathers face today and offers hope and practical help. You'll find encouragement from Jim Daly to work hard at becoming a better dad.

Dr. Kevin Leman, *New York Times* bestselling
author of *Be the Dad She Needs You to Be*

Jim Daly not only leads the organization called Focus on the Family, but he's truly focused on *his* family. This book comes out of experience, know-how, wisdom, expertise, and a deep understanding of the power of fatherhood, both temporally and eternally. *The Good Dad* should be required reading for every parent around the world!

Brad Lomenick, adviser and brand ambassador
for Catalyst and author of *The Catalyst Leader*

The absence of fathers is one of the major problems in America today, but to that must be added the problem that many fathers actually do not know how to father. Jim Daly is just the right man to write this book, helping all men to understand what it means to be a faithful, stronger, more caring father. Not only is he one of America's leading experts in family life; he writes from *his own experience.* I have seen Jim in action as a father, and because of that, I'm led to commend this book to every-one. It needs to be in the hands of every man, in order that he can become the father he was meant to be.

Dr. R. Albert Mohler Jr., president
of The Southern Baptist Theological Seminary,
Louisville, Kentucky

Jim Daly is one of our most trusted, authentic experts when it comes to families. As a father myself, I wholeheartedly recommend *The Good Dad* to fathers with children of any age as a valuable resource for growing and sustaining a healthy family.

Dr. Tony Evans, founder and president
of The Urban Alternative and senior pastor
of Oak Cliff Bible Fellowship, Dallas Texas

Jim's message is a critical one for all dads. It reminds us that there are no perfect dads, yet provides hope that all of us can make a difference in the lives of our children. This book will encourage any dad.

Brian Blomberg, chief development officer,
National Center for Fathering

The
Good Dad

Becoming *the* Father You
Were Meant to Be

JIM DALY

WITH PAUL ASAY

ZONDERVAN

The Good Dad
Copyright © 2014 by James Daly

This title is also available as a Zondervan ebook.
Visit www.zondervan.com/ebooks.

Requests for information should be addressed to:
Zondervan, 3900 *Sparks Drive SE, Grand Rapids, Michigan 49546*

Library of Congress Cataloging-in-Publication Data

Daly, Jim, 1961–
    The good dad : becoming the father you were meant to be / Jim Daly,
    with Paul Asay. — 1st [edition].
        pages cm
        ISBN 978-0-310-33179-7 (softcover)
        1. Fatherhood — Religious aspects — Christianity. 2. Fathers — Religious
life. I. Title.
    BV4529.17.D35   2014
    248.8'421—dc23   2013047062

Cover design: Studio Gearbox
Cover photography: Thinkstock®
Interior design: Beth Shagene

Printed in the United States of America

---

14 15 16 17 18 19 /DCI/ 20 19 18 17 16 15 14 13 12 11 10 9 8 7 6 5 4 3 2 1

I dedicate this book to my two boys, Trent and Troy.
Our laughter together is a melody of love
I will cherish and remember for the rest of my life.
I am beyond proud to be your dad.

Contents

One

Moments

It was Dad's Night in Yucca Valley.

It came like clockwork every year to that hot, dusty California town. The Yucca Valley football team would line the field before a game, each player separated by two or three yards of grass. I was a sophomore, and this was my first Dad's Night. We faced the home stands, bleachers full of moms and dads and brothers and sisters. The bright lights of the stadium made us squint.

Normally, I relished standing under those lights. I had always felt pretty comfortable on that field, one of the few places where I ever felt truly at home. But in that moment, on Dad's Night, they felt too bright. I felt exposed, embarrassed. I knew what was coming. Right then, in that moment, I wanted to be somewhere else, anywhere else. I wanted time to jump ahead ten minutes so I could strap on my helmet, grab the football, and do what I knew how to do.

One by one, the announcer called out the name of a father. The dad would run into the lights and onto the field, jogging through the grass to stand by his son — a small celebration, a way to acknowledge the dads who had helped their kids throw a football or taught them how to tackle or made sure they didn't miss practices. Not everyone had a dad there, of course. But back in 1976, we had a lot more intact families than we do today. And those who didn't have a father around typically invited someone else to stand in his place — a brother or grandfather or friend.

But that night, I didn't have anyone. I had forgotten to get someone to play my "Dad," just for that one night.

"Jim Daly," the announcer said over the loudspeaker, and then a pause. "Jim Daly's father is not present tonight." Boom, that was it. Down the row it went. I watched as other fathers ran onto the field to hug or shake hands with their sons. And there I stood, alone again.

Want to know how important fathers are? Ask the guy who didn't have one.

Vanishing Dads

When it comes right down to it, life is a series of moments — bite-size chunks of time that help define us and shape our view of the world around us. Sometimes you know what they look like *in* the moment. Sometimes you barely notice them until weeks or months or years later. But then one day, you'll look back on them and realize how important they were. And maybe you'll say, like I sometimes do, "That was something special. Something critical. That was a *moment.*"

We all have moments connected with our fathers, stories that not only helped illustrate what kind of men our own dads were, but maybe point to what they should've been. And like it or not, those moments shape how we think about fatherhood itself. Sometimes they can set the bar for us, show us what it means to be a dad. Sometimes they can serve as cautionary tales — *Man, I never want to act* that *way, the way my old man did after a few too many beers.* Or maybe, like my Dad's Night moment, they set themselves apart by their very absence, for the vacuum they left behind.

Every year I struggled with trying to figure out what to do for Dad's Night. Every year, I thought, *Crap, who can I bring?* Every year, I had to scrounge up a substitute "Dad" to fill in for the real fathers who failed me. My biological father essentially drank himself to death. My stepfather left the day we buried my mother, literally taking a taxi out of my family's life with barely a good-bye. And my foster father ... well, for now, let's just call him a little odd. And every one of them had left my life by the time I turned twelve.

You'll hear more about those men in due time. But for now, you just need to know that I had to deal with the awkwardness I so keenly felt that Dad's Night in one way or another almost every day while growing up. I always felt an empty space on the field.

I know I'm nothing special. My experience has become almost the norm.

According to recent United States Census figures, fifteen million kids live apart from their biological fathers. That's one out of every three American children.[1] When we look at the rate of fatherlessness among African-Americans, that rate soars to two out of every three.[2] Some people call it an epidemic. Back in 1976, I might've had three teammates who didn't have dads there on Dad's Night. I doubt Yucca Valley High School still honors fathers every season anymore, but if it did? That number would probably hover closer to twenty-five or thirty.

But while growing up without a father has become far more common today, that doesn't make it any easier.

Instinctively, we know this. In a recent poll by the National Center for Fathering, 92 percent of respondents said that dads make a "unique contribution" to the lives of their children, and seven out of ten see absentee dads as the biggest family or social problem facing the United States.[3] Research backs up such a belief. About 44 percent of children in mother-only households live in poverty, according to a 2011 U.S. Census study, compared to 12 percent of children living in intact homes.[4] These kids will more likely have trouble with alcohol or drugs, says the National Fatherhood Initiative. They're more likely to cause trouble in school or have run-ins with the law. And after their high school-playing days end, these boys without fathers have (according to a Bureau of Justice Statistics Special Report) a higher likelihood of landing in jail.[5]

The stats for girls are no better. They, too, struggle as kids and into adulthood. Moreover, females raised without fathers are four times more likely to engage in sexual intercourse at an early age, and more than twice as likely to get pregnant early.[6]

If you look at virtually any measure of the mental and emotional health of children and how they make the transition into adulthood, kids with involved dads simply do better.

I find it ironic that my teammates so long ago didn't always appreciate those fathers running out onto the field. In the locker room after practice, I'd listen to them complain about their dads — the rules, the curfews, the fights. They'd say, "My dad's a pain in the [you know what]." And as I'd listen, I'd think, *If you only knew.*

At the time, I lived with my brother, Dave, a guy barely old enough to buy beer. While he certainly was a good brother and gave me some much-needed stability, I didn't see him as

a father figure. He set few boundaries, established few rules
— a situation some of my friends would've loved. Curfew? Of
course not.

On fall Friday nights as I walked out the door for my football game, I'd ask, "What time do you want me to come home?"

"Oh, two, three in the morning should be fine," he'd say.

"Well, okay," I remember saying. "I'll *try* to stay out that late."

I never felt jealous of my teammates — at least that I
remember. But I did feel a sense of loss in talking with the
other kids who had a father, even if they had a strained relationship. I remember the yearning: *If you only knew what I'd
do to have a dad to be there to talk with or to set a curfew. If you
only knew how much I want a dad to have a rough time with. If
you only knew.*

Jeff Shook, my teammate and close friend, gave me the
only real window into what a "normal" family looked like.
He'd sometimes invite me over for a pregame meal. Mrs. Shook
would cook us some steaks and baked potatoes, all the protein
and carbohydrates you need before a game. On some pregame
days, Mr. Shook would show up too, and we'd spend the meal
just talking and laughing. And I could see a glimmer of what
I'd been missing.

When Jeff and I got back in touch years later, he learned
something about my backstory, something I had kept pretty
private until recently.

"I had no idea all that stuff was going on in your life," he
told me. "If I would've known, I think our family would've
done more to help you." But I didn't want that. I didn't want to
be a project. I just wanted to go over and have a meal with Jeff.
I never said, *Man, I wish I had a mom and dad like you.* I never
went there. I never opened that door.

The dads in my life didn't teach me much, but I learned

a few things from them anyway. I developed mechanisms to cope — the ability to laugh at myself and at life's ups and downs. The ability to move on after disappointment. And I certainly learned that I couldn't rely on anyone else for much of anything. No father would hug me after the game and tell me I played well, win or lose. No dad would tell me he felt proud of me. *Ah, who needs a dad anyway?* I'd tell myself.

But then, in moments like Dad's Night, I knew how great it would feel to have a father with me, to stand beside me, on that grassy field.

On nights like those, it felt like someone tossed another rock for me to lug around in my backpack. And then I'd just shrug and keep on going.

Praise, Laments, and Complications

When I was five, my father came home drunk and threatened to kill my mom, and I didn't see him again for years. When I was seven, another man, Hank, came into my life and became my stepfather a year later. But when I was nine, my mother died, and Hank left too, deserting me and my brothers and sisters. I went to live with a foster family named the Reils after that, but that situation only lasted a year, and things went sour well before then. My father and I gave it another shot when I was eleven, but that also failed because of his drinking. After that, I stopped trying to find a good dad. It didn't seem like one was in the cards for me.

Some people find it ironic that a guy who had such a dysfunctional childhood would go on to become president of Focus on the Family. But as I look back on it, I think my brokenness as a child gave me the passion to help others build their own strong families. I wanted to come alongside people and help them avoid what I experienced. I didn't connect the dots the moment I signed up with Focus. I didn't consciously say to myself, *Let's save people the pain and heartache I suffered.* But I knew the importance of family. And why? Because I never had a great family of my own as a child, and I knew I had missed out on some pretty important stuff. I know the critical importance of fathers, because I know how important they could've been to me if only they'd shown up.

And our constituents constantly reconfirm for me the importance of fathers. I hear their stories — their *moments* — almost every day.

Not long ago, I wrote a blog post titled "Should Father's Day Be Outlawed?" in which I reflected on a push by some to eliminate the holiday. Readers, not too surprisingly perhaps, said we should keep the holiday. They'd bring up the shared times fishing or tinkering on the family car. They'd mention little nuggets of wisdom their dads passed on to them. They'd write about how much they learned from their fathers as they went about their daily business, working and praying and living.

Consider these thoughts from David:

> *In the eighth grade I played on what I'd generously call a not very good school football team. I was not a star. I played center. We played a team in a really not very nice neighborhood and it was pouring rain and the field was not good — not much grass and mostly mud. And my dad was there before the game to see me warm up and was there when it was over, standing in his suit with an umbrella, cheering us all the way. We lost the football game, but my dad showed me I was a winner in his book.*

Breana wrote:

> *He read to me, he played with me, he taught me about*

nature and life and how to ride a bike. He's the one who taught me to drive on the freeway, the one who showed me how to use a rifle and then took me hunting. He's the one who listens to my ideas and dreams, spends hours researching how to make them happen, creates a flowchart and checklist, and helps me to turn them into realities ... He waits up for me during my late night babysitting jobs, even if he got up at 4:30 and drove halfway across the state that day.

From Brian:

What I remember most about my dad is that when I was a kid, he always had oil-stained hands ... That might not seem terribly significant to a lot of people, and it might not be fashionable to have grease under your fingernails, but that is the way my dad approaches life. He often works long after his hands are dirty or bloody or bruised from whatever task he has undertaken. He was hands-on and involved in what is important to his children and his grandchildren. When we played baseball or soccer, he coached. When I was in Boy Scouts, he was a leader. In church youth group, he chaperoned. When my brother worked on cars, he was under the hood. When we rode motorcycles, he tuned them up. When I became a police officer, he listened to my stories. When I received awards, he came to watch. When I graduated from law school, he celebrated with me. When our children were born, he was the first one we called and he is the one we trust to love and encourage them as their "Pop-Pop." In those times, the hands of my dad have held me when I cried, picked me up when I fell, patted my back when I did right, spanked my bottom when I did wrong, applauded my accomplishments when I succeeded at anything worth doing. Just recently, I felt the most incredible peace when I found out my dad's hands prayed for me as well.

Think dads don't make a difference? The more than three hundred comments sparked by this blog beg to differ. They can make a huge difference and change a child's life for the better. Over and over, respondents used words like *hero* and *role model* to describe their dads. Some called their fathers the most precious, most influential people in their lives.

But other readers used different words to describe their dads — *demanding, legalistic, busy, abusive*. Some reminded me of my own sad experiences. They talked of fathers who left them when they were very young. Or fathers who drank too much. Or fathers who kicked them out of the house when they were sixteen. They lamented their fathers' poor choices and acknowledged broken relationships. Some say that on Father's Day they send cards to their uncles or grandfathers or mothers — the people who served them as better fathers than their real dads ever did.

And people would often express the inherent complexity, the messiness, that's part of being a family. *My father wasn't perfect, but . . .* they'd begin. Or, *My dad didn't have much time for us, but . . .* Or, *My father made some bad choices when I was younger, but . . .*

People wrote about how their dads did really well in one area but faltered in another. They'd talk about how their fathers didn't really know how to be fathers until something happened in their lives to change them, often a moment that involved Christ's influence on them. Sometimes readers admitted that they rebelled as teens and their relationship soured, only to get redeemed later in life.

And that brings up an important point that we'll hammer over and over as we talk about what it means to be a father, and what it takes to be a good one. Yes, fathers are incredibly important. Yes, what fathers do impact their kids mightily, for good or for ill. But *all* of us will fail sometimes. *All* of us will fall short. I know I do. My own two boys, Trent and Troy, know as well as anyone how I sometimes fall short — and I'm president of Focus on the Family! I'm *writing a book* about fatherhood. We need to cut ourselves some slack. We can't grow so intimidated by the job that we kick ourselves for every minor misstep or freeze up and stop trying altogether.

I also believe that even if you had a less than ideal upbringing, as I did, you can overcome it. You don't need to feel burdened with the sins of your father — not if you learn from his failures and commit to overcoming them.

Not having a reliable father affected me mightily. I think I would've been healthier with one. I would've had a greater sense of confidence. I would've had a place to go where I could talk through my concerns and issues. Just having conversations with a dad might've helped me make better decisions, particularly in high school. A dad might've helped me make choices I knew in my heart were right but just needed some reinforcement to actually make them.

But in a way, I think I'm a better father because of what I went through — not a perfect father, but a better father because of what I *didn't* get. I know the ache in my heart of not having a dad in the moment I needed him. So with my boys, I want to deliver that, to give them what I didn't have. I still fall short. I'm not perfect. But I know they get a good part of me.

There's hope. You don't have to remain tied to your father's legacy if you had a poor one. You don't have to stay anchored to his shortcomings. You can become something better. We can get better at this fatherhood thing. Our kids aren't asking for perfection. They're asking for our *presence* — to show up for the job each and every day. They're asking us to be there for them, to guide them, to hug them, and sometimes to just stand on the sidelines — ready to run onto the field when our name gets called.

And when you're present, truly *with them* as they grow up, you find the opportunity to create bonds with your kids that will stick with them — and you — for a lifetime. That boy will always remember that summer when Dad taught him to cast a lure. That girl will always remember those afternoons when Dad played catch with her. Those things *stick*. They're moments. And lives worth living are made up of those moments.

Rocking into Fatherhood

In late 1999, my wife, Jean, and I had been trying to get pregnant for a while.

Simple task, right? Well, at the time it seemed easier said than done, given the fact that I served as vice president for Focus on the Family's international division, traveling all over the world. I remember the week of conception. I'd just returned from a trip to Asia and had two weeks at home over Thanksgiving before I had to leave again. During those two weeks, we struck gold, obviously; but when Jean told me the news that she was pregnant, the hectic time made it feel almost matter-of-fact. Almost like we'd completed a task on our to-do list. *Boom, we can check that off. Success! Fertilization has occurred.* I didn't feel much like a father yet. Everything felt abstract, theoretical.

Fast-forward nine months. All the abstraction has vanished. Things have become *real* in a big way. Jean's been in labor for twenty-seven hours and feels utterly exhausted. The baby's vitals don't look good. The doctors prepare to do a C-section, but they give her one last chance to push. And God bless her, on that last push — maybe because she really wants to avoid that C-section — she gets it done. Trent comes into this world around 4:30 p.m. on August 12, 2000. They clean him up and bring him back to us, all swaddled and shiny. The nurses want him to stay in the birthing room, but Jean is just wiped out and ready to sleep.

So at about 8:00 p.m., I take Trent — tiny, helpless baby — and together we sit in the rocking chair. And there we spend the night, all night, in the rocking chair.

It feels incredible, that time with Trent, holding that precious little life literally in my hands. *Oh man, I'm a dad*, I think. *I'm really a dad.* And in that moment, all the joys and duties and responsibilities of fatherhood hit me for the first time. I rock him through the night, the chair gliding back and forth almost silently as Jean sleeps beside us. And as I rock, I talk. I pray. "I hope I can be a good father to you," I say. "I hope I can be a better father, the father I never had."

I didn't sleep that night. If I did doze off, I did so for just a second or two. I couldn't get over having this tiny being in my arms. I didn't *want* to fall asleep. Didn't want to accidentally drop him or let him slip from my arms. I wanted to hold him, to protect him, to keep him close all through the night.

What a beautiful night! For me, it amounted to a metamorphosis into fatherhood — physically, mentally, emotionally, spiritually.

Call it a moment.

─────────────── **TO THINK ABOUT** ───────────────

1. What sorts of moments do you remember about your dad? What are the positive ones? What are the negative ones?

2. Did your dad do some things — teach you some skills, pass on some lessons, have fun with you — that you have replicated, or you'd like to replicate, with your own children?

3. Are there aspects of your dad that you do your best to avoid?

4. What sorts of moments are you making for your own children?

5. Is there a moment you remember when you truly understood what being a father meant?

Two
___

The Look of a Father

"I can't deal with this. I'm moving back to San Francisco."

With those words, my stepfather, Hank, greeted us after my siblings and I returned home from our mom's funeral — a funeral he didn't attend. They were the last words I ever heard him say.

While Mike, Dave, Kim, Dee Dee, and I said our mortal farewells to Mom, Hank had started packing. By the time we returned from the funeral, our house had been almost completely emptied — no TV; no green couch; no pictures on the wall. Our clothes had been dumped from dressers and left in piles around the house. A few of our personal belongings dotted the floor — some toys of mine in a box, perhaps a snapshot or two. Anything of real value, anything Hank considered valuable, had disappeared, either sold or shipped off. And now he was leaving too. He carried a pair of suitcases to the curb in the twilight. A taxicab was waiting. And just like that, he fled. I never saw him again.

He didn't bother to wave good-bye. He never even turned around.

I can't deal with this. Funny, since Hank looked like he could deal with anything. He resembled Liam Neeson — a big, handsome guy with a chiseled nose and blondish hair. He was probably around fifty, I'd guess. Navy guy. A sailor. We called him "Hank the Tank," and he could be pretty brutal. Not physically (not to me, anyway), but he intimidated us and got angry pretty easily. He'd never married before, never had children. And although he could scare the stuffing out of us "children" (Mike was grown, and Dave nearly so), he actually *didn't* know how to "deal with" us. You could tell he didn't love the kids at all. He considered the five of us just excess baggage, the kids he had to put up with to be with my mom.

But his passion, at least for my mom, ran deep.

They started dating when I was seven and got married a year later. He knew that all my brothers and sisters, much older than me, would leave the house in a few years. Hank probably figured he could wait. After all, he and my mom would have the rest of their lives to spend with each other.

And then my mom got sick. I had no context for how bad it was, and no one really told me. Hank never did. But he isolated her from us. She slept in the back bedroom, and Hank would literally lock the door to keep us away from her. Maybe he was worried we'd tire her or make her anxious about us. I'd go weeks without seeing her.

One day when I came home from school, I saw the door open a crack, something that hardly ever happened. I knew I'd make Hank angry if I went in, but when I walked over to the door, she called me.

"I'm glad it's you," my mom said, and she invited me in.

The sight of her took my breath away. She was so skinny, so frail. Her hair, normally reddish-brown and shoulder length, had been cut incredibly short. I had never seen her like that.

But she still smiled like my mother. She asked if I could do a favor for her — go to the store, buy some chrysanthemum seeds, and plant them under her window.

I didn't know then that I wasn't really doing *her* the favor, but she was doing *me* one. She knew those beautiful flowers would remind me of her.

With my mom so sick, Hank got forced into the role of a single father. And he didn't know what to do, even if he *wanted* to do it. He filled our house with rules and regulations and lots of discipline, but no love that I ever felt. If I left a coat lying on the sofa, he'd force me to hang it up fifty or a hundred times. But he never hugged us, never asked us how we felt. And while he'd at least take the time to yell at my more rebellious brothers and sisters, he didn't pay much attention to me at all.

He did perform one duty that should've made us feel more like a family. Most nights, he made us dinner. And though he never prayed before my mom got sick, he'd pray now. We'd huddle around the dinner table and hold hands.

"Dear Lord," he'd say. And sometimes that would be as far as he'd get before he'd begin to convulse and shake with gut-wrenching, silent sobs.

Keep in mind that I didn't know what was going on with my mother or why Hank suddenly got religion. I didn't know how sick she was. I certainly had no idea she was *dying.* Hank didn't talk to any of us about her. And so when Hank started shaking over a dinner blessing, part of me thought, *This guy's a wacko.* None of us kids knew exactly what to make of it. I'm ashamed to say it, but when we saw him shake at the table, we'd giggle. We all thought the same thing: *This loser of a stepdad is losing his mind.*

Looking back, I see the bigger picture. Hank probably knew my mom didn't have much time left. And sitting there at the table, praying to a God he barely understood, surrounded by kids and responsibilities he barely knew, all of his worry, frustration, and sorrow just poured out of him. *What am I going to do?* Even then, he probably thought, *I can't handle this.*

Flustered Fathers

"I can't deal with this," Hank had said. I wonder how many guys have thought the same thing when they heard their girlfriend was pregnant. Or as they check out of the hospital with a new baby. A long night filled with colicky cries. After another call from the principal's office. Or at 2:00 a.m., when their teenage daughter is *still* not home.

I can't deal with this.

"It is much easier to become a father than to be one," wrote author Kent Nerburn, and every dad knows he speaks the truth.[7] Hank the Tank never wanted to be a father. But even for men who'd *like* to do the job, it can feel pretty intimidating. We can master what we do for a living or dominate on the basketball court. But so much of what we experience as fathers, we can't control. When our six-month-old baby starts wailing, we can't *make* him stop. When our son is failing algebra, we can't *make* him pass. When our daughter gets bullied, we can't just magically *make* everything all better. Fatherhood doesn't much resemble being a mechanic: We can't fix things with a turn of a socket wrench. It's much slower work. Subtle work. Sometimes we don't know if what we're doing is even working. For men, that can feel very frustrating.

And then there's the added difficulty of trying to figure out what it means to be a father today, because the role has changed significantly. According to a Pew Research Study, 63 percent of dads say it's more difficult to raise children today than it was even a generation ago.[8] Things have changed so much that many men don't even know the job requirements.

Fatherhood indeed looked a lot different a century or so ago. When agriculture dominated our society, most men worked from dawn till dusk in the fields. Their jobs were to provide and protect. Up to a certain age, childrearing remained mostly Mom's work, and the children's chores often kept them near hearth and home — sweeping floors, washing dishes, feeding the chickens, and the like.

But as the child grew, he or she often gradually moved outside the safer confines of home and into the wider world of Dad. He'd teach them how to hunt and fish. He'd train them how to use a hammer and saw so they could help patch fences or build new outbuildings. Although this pattern especially held true for boys, girls also worked alongside their dads. And on family farms and in rural areas across the country, that still remains true today. A friend of mine who grew up on a farm knew how to do pretty much everything that needed doing by the time he celebrated his fourteenth birthday — plowing fields, milking cows, running the farm equipment, even helping to birth calves. It was hard work, and sometimes each chore could take hours of sweaty labor. That gave kids a lot of time to think. A lot of time to talk. And that's when Dad would really come into his own as a father. As he and his children worked shoulder to shoulder, he'd talk with them about keeping their word, keeping their bonds — all the values that meant something in that environment.

Those values got transferred from one generation to the next very organically, very naturally, almost as a by-product — or maybe, more fairly, an extension — of the father's two primary duties: providing for the family (with food, money, and a few lifelong lessons) and protecting the family (from poverty or outside dangers or even in-family delinquency). The dad was the family's strong man and traditionally its ultimate authority. While women were just as important to the family's well-being (and sometimes worked in the field just as hard as the men), their traditional duties centered on nurturing. Caregiving. Keeping everything running smoothly.

Now fast-forward to the twenty-first century and take a look at the typical "traditional" family. Not many of us live on a farm. More often than not, both parents work outside the home. The problems and dangers we face are often more subtle, more insidious, than a flash flood or a bear outside the door. And while we still have a huge need for a nurturing, caregiving force inside the home — the traditional role of a mother — a father's traditional duties have undergone a huge transformation. His duties as a provider have been split between parents. His duties as a protector have grown less obvious. Kids don't have to work alongside Dad when they reach a certain age, robbing Dad of valuable lesson and bonding time.

More mothers than ever have embarked on solid, lucrative careers. Women now make up almost half of the labor force (47 percent in 2010, according to statistics from the United States Department of Labor).[9] A report by the Council of Graduate Schools found that women outnumber men in graduate degree work, 58 to 42 percent.[10] And a study by Pew Research found that women spend twice as much time working for pay as they did in 1965, while, conversely, men spend twice as many hours doing household chores and watching the kids.[11]

None of these statistics are, in themselves, good or bad. But they do illustrate the radical time of transition that fathers find themselves in right now.

On the one hand, I think fathers face a higher and greater expectation to be more engaged with their children. With more moms pitching in as "providers," we expect dads to be better nurturers and caregivers. We change diapers and cook breakfast and kiss boo-boos. And that's great — fantastic, in fact. But guys don't always feel at home in those areas.

On the other hand, our culture often sees dads as next to irrelevant. We're sperm donors, and that's it. According to the National Fatherhood Initiative, 31 percent of children who live without their fathers haven't seen their dads at all in the last three months.[12] And even fathers who stick around get told they provide comic relief more than anything. Flip on the television during prime time and you'll almost certainly see a few clueless, buffoonish dads dragging their knuckles across the screen. It doesn't matter if you watch a sitcom or a pizza commercial — while mothers usually appear as the wise, practical, thinking parent, fathers blunder in just as oversized kids.

On the one hand, we dads hear we have to do *everything*, and do it perfectly. On the other hand, we're good for *nothing*. No wonder we feel confused. Our jobs have morphed from a family's primary provider into something else not nearly as well-defined. We hear that we'll probably fail at that anyway, and therefore many guys seem to say, "Why even try?"

Most of us can't go back to the farm. And I believe that, as fathers, we should rejoice in the fact that we can take a greater role in raising our own kids. I see more engaged fathers as a great trend. But even great trends come with their share of obstacles. And I think some of the stuff that made us great fathers a century ago can explain why we sometimes struggle with what we're supposed to be today.

The Hero Gene

All men have what scientists call the SRY gene, responsible for growing the male testes. For a long time, science believed this gene had no other purpose — until some Australian scientists took a closer look in 2012 and discovered it also plays a part in how men react to stress. In stressful situations, the SRY gene triggers increased blood flow to a man's major organs and releases more of a chemical called catecholamine, both of which factor into our classic "fight or flight" response.[13]

Women, who lack the SRY gene, react much differently under stress. Their bodies generate internal opiates that help control pain, among other things. It may make females less prone to aggression but more apt to engage in what researchers call a "tend and befriend" response.

These scientists didn't use their findings to draw any conclusions on parental tendencies, but it's no big leap to make from the SRY gene to some of the trends we see in families today. Mothers tend to the kids while the fathers either take off, get abusive, or hide out in their man caves playing video games (a curious combination of fight *and* flight).

We need to tread lightly before we make sweeping generalizations about how men and women do or should behave. There are many, many exceptions. Even as we talk about deadbeat dads, we know many deadbeat moms exist too. Many men out there either overcame their SRY programming or channeled it in such a way as to become great caregivers. In 2013, the Pew Research Center declared that the number of single-father households has grown ninefold since 1960.[14]

But while fathers head about 24 percent of single-parent households,[15] single mothers still make up a sizable majority — and I think they always will. Parenthood tends to come instinctually to women in ways that infrequently characterize men.

Women have become the bedrock of the modern-day family. They're predictable. Dependable. Nurturing. They have a desire to take care of things and people. When you see a woman who loves her family, you see something *normal*. Men are the wild cards. And the same gene that made us such effective protectors in days gone by may make us more prone to bail out.

Family life produces a lot of stress, but of a different sort than what we're wired to deal with. We're ready for action — to protect, to save. The SRY gene primes us to "fight" when danger looms. When disaster hits, most guys respond well. Fewer men shrink back from *that* moment. It's instinctive.

Back in my college days, some classmates and I took a trip to the Grand Canyon. We walked by this guy sitting at a picnic bench, pumping a kerosene lamp, and before we moved twenty feet past him, I heard an explosion. I turned around and saw the guy sprawled out on the ground, totally knocked out from the blast. His flaming kerosene lamp was spinning near the base of a tree *completely covered in dry leaves*. It looked like it might light up like a torch at any second. So, boom, I ripped off my jacket, ran over to the lamp, and in one swoop — *thwap!* — put out the fire. It was awesome. And for the next, oh, thirty seconds or so, the people around me seemed pretty impressed.

I think most guys would react like that. When we know what we need to do, most of us are pretty good about doing it. We want to protect. We want to save. We want to do something *big*. Why do you think superhero movies have become so popular? Why do you think our televisions air so many shows about catching the bad guys or saving lives or protecting our communities? Something in these shows appeals to a man's sense of justice. We want to band together, do good things, protect our communities and our families. We want to be the hero or be with a group of guys willing to be heroes.

But as a dad, you don't have many of those transcendent, hero-like moments: *Let's go mow the lawn! Let's go rake up the leaves! Let's have a tea party! Yeah! Awesome!* This is not the stuff of blockbuster movies or prime-time crime dramas. Maybe in days gone by, men could guard the old homestead from wolves or desperados, standing by the window with gun in hand. Now we protect our kids from bad Internet sites and trans-fats. We ask our wives whether the kids can have a sundae tonight.

Don't get me wrong. It's good to protect your family from all sorts of modern-day perils. But how different life looks now than a hundred years ago! The "fight" in our SRY gene doesn't get as much of a chance to stretch. But the "flight" part of the gene always stands ready to kick in. And because of that, men often leave their battles instead of engaging in them. They run away.

Performance Anxiety

For most men, a big part of who we are is rooted in performance. We judge ourselves by how well we do on the playing field or in our jobs. We keep score.

No wonder fatherhood feels so scary for most of us. Our job title as "Dad" seems confusing and muddled. We can't be the heroes we see in our imagination. Sometimes we don't even know what it means to be a father. We sometimes don't know who our kids need us to be. Lots of us had fathers who were poor role models. We feel inadequate.

All those factors scream potential failure. "I don't think I'm the right guy," we'll say. "I don't think I'm good enough. I don't think I know how to handle a crisis. I feel fearful. I feel fear in me." Men don't like these feelings of fear and uncertainty. They freak us out. And they make some of us want to run away, like a little boy.

It reminds me of my high school football days. I had some pretty good quarterback skills, and on the football field, I felt like I could take care of business. I knew what I was supposed to do, and I had a fair dose of confidence that I could do it. I felt in control of my destiny, that I could rise above the competition and win.

But outside of that arena, I felt completely inadequate. I see that as another common trait of men — that feeling of being able to perform well in certain areas but coming up totally inadequate in others. You go through your teen years feeling that you're not handsome enough or smart enough or big enough, or that you have too many pimples. You see yourself as not very capable.

As a freshman in high school, I stood around in gym class behind a guy named Glen and one of his buddies. Now, Glen's family produced a lot of great swimmers — I think one brother went to the Olympics — and all of them were these huge, muscular guys. Glen, two years older than me, was no exception. So there we all stood by the gym wall, with me trying to hide behind Glen as much as I could. I wanted to be invisible — me in my funky little trunks and Converse sneakers. I didn't want anybody to notice me. I could vaguely hear Glen and his friend talking about something as they stood in front of me, but I didn't pay much attention, until out of nowhere, Glen wheeled around, took the palm of his hand, and — *bam!* He hit me right in the chest. I literally heard the bone crack.

And then I realized that Glen and his buddy had been

talking about *me*. His sternum jab was just his way, I guess, of violently pointing.

"See this guy? He hasn't really filled out yet," Glen said. "He's kind of like a twig." And they went on talking about how bodies change and guys get bigger as they get older. I felt like a science experiment, a lab specimen. Glen was just using me to prove a point. He didn't want to pick a fight; he just wanted to use me as a frog. I had nowhere to go with that.

Before long, I became the school's quarterback, and I filled out okay. And yet the insecurities of that one single moment stayed with me for a very long time.

I think almost every guy has messages of inadequacy. Rolling around inside us, we hear these messages that we don't measure up. And those messages get constantly reinforced in the culture.

If we're honest with ourselves, many of us feel the same inadequacies when it comes to fatherhood. I know I did. Even as I rocked Trent back and forth on the night of his birth, I felt rocked with doubt. I'd never had a good father, a dad I'd consider a role model. Would I fall down, just like my own dads did? I'd think, *Do I have what it takes? Yes? No?* And my answer almost had two halves. On one side — the competitive, football-playing side — I was like, *Yeah, I'll get it done. I'll do it.* The quarterback side of me thought, *We'll score a touchdown. Come on, guys. We're going to score a touchdown!* But behind all that huddled those massive doubts and insecurities. *Will we? Can I? Will I?*

The Secret of Fatherhood

We all have insecurities boiling inside us. Our culture tells us incessantly what failures we are as fathers. Even our own genes can throw up roadblocks. We don't get to be the heroes we feel like we should be. And so we fail. We lose interest. We'd rather play video games.

But we can't. We have to push aside those fears and insecurities and our own laziness — the "ways of childhood" the apostle Paul talks about (1 Corinthians 13:11). We have to transcend our own weaknesses and predilections and become the greater man. I think God calls us to do just that.

"For the flesh desires what is contrary to the Spirit, and the Spirit what is contrary to the flesh. They are in conflict with each other, so that you are not to do whatever you want," writes Paul in Galatians 5:17.

Sometimes we might wonder why our flesh and our Spirit always seem to be in such opposition. After all, God created both our bodies and souls. But I think the Lord sets up paradoxes in life in order to create environments for us to learn how to become more like him, situations that push against our natural inclinations and into a more God-honoring stance. It pushes us out of our comfort zone and forces us to lean on him more and more.

I like to think of it like this. We all live, in a sense, in boxes, with the whole box of life tilted in God's direction. We can fight, we can struggle, we can deny him, we can scream. We can do whatever to try to move away from him. But the elevation of the box on one side keeps cranking up until we reach a tipping point. Something snaps, and we fall to the other side. It's all about leaning into God.

Marriage thrusts us into such a box. You're selfish? You like calling your own shots? Get married. And if you're selfish too long, you're not going to be married long. You have to start giving.

Fatherhood is exactly the same thing. If some selfishness

remains in you after marriage, then have some kids — and be responsible for them. Sure, you can have children all day long, as many men do, and have no accountability. But if you have a sense of responsibility for that child, you take up that mantle. Yes, it will be hard. You will not know how to deal with them very well, at least at first. You'll feel scared. You'll feel frustrated. It's hard because, in some ways, God knows it has to be hard for us. Only through that pain and difficulty do we grow ever more like him. Our flawed flesh and scared souls may give us pause. But according to Paul, "the Spirit God gave us does not make us timid, but gives us power, love and self-discipline" (2 Timothy 1:7).

And that, in the end, is the heart of it all, the secret of fatherhood — living in power, love, and self-discipline. Sometimes that goes against our instincts or what we'd like. But that's what God calls us to.

And at the center of it all, as Paul once again says, is *love*. Always hopeful, always trusting, always persevering. As a father, love is the key, the secret to everything. It's not rocket science. It's pretty easy, really. If you love your kids and you can show them that you love them, everything else falls into place.

And we need to love them as a *father*. We can't mother our children; most of our children already have great mothers. Don't be their mother. Be their dad. And what does it mean to be their dad? It means you do have to connect. Engage them in the way that you can. Be natural with it. Cut loose a little. It will come naturally to you. Turtles know what to do. Penguins know what to do. Other animals know what to do as dads. We human fathers know what to do too. Sure, circumstances have changed. Most of us can't talk about life with our boys while working in the fields anymore. But we can find opportunities, if we only look for them.

I mentioned earlier that many men don't even know the job requirements of fatherhood. But fatherhood's not a job, and it never has been. Being a father isn't something we *do*. It's something we *are*. That's hard for us to understand sometimes, being as task oriented as we are. But I think that's what Paul is getting at. We need to lean on love, push beyond our instincts, and go deeper. We don't set aside being a good dad when we're off the clock. It's something we become. And just as we're always in the process of unpacking our faith, growing ever closer to Jesus long after we become Christians, so the road to becoming a father is a never-ending journey. We're always learning how to be a good dad. We're always in the process of becoming one. And we never cast aside that process.

A Father's Love

We talk about our moms as the center of the family. And in certain critical ways, they always will be.

But as fathers we have just as important a role to play in the lives of our boys and girls that goes beyond carrying the family's mantle of leadership. We must get back to the father's traditional roles of provision and protection. A picture comes to my mind — a big, old tree in the backyard, an oak that spreads its branches across the sky like open arms, an oak that kids filled with energy run to in the morning or sit beside for comfort in the afternoon. I think of that feeling of unshakeable security, that sense of always being there for you.

Just the other day I had a conversation with Troy, our youngest son. We planned to attend a play late that afternoon, a play he'd been looking forward to, but he wasn't feeling well. He had a bad head cold and sounded like he could use some chicken noodle soup and good rest.

"Are you sure you want to go?" I asked him.

"Oh, I *do* want to see it," he said.

"Well, you want to sit next to me so I can put my arm around you?" I asked. "Would that make you feel better?"

His whole countenance brightened. "Yeah!" he said.

That's a pretty special feeling as a father, knowing your hug is as good, or as healing, in a way, as a bowl of chicken noodle soup. And even though that sounds very nurturing and motherly, I see it more as that old oak tree, always there to provide and protect.

When I think of what it means to be a dad, I think of a jolly father who says, "Come, come and sit on my lap. My boy, what did you do today? Did you make a mistake today? How did that go? What did you learn from that?" That may sound funny, but that's the dad figure to me, a reflection of how I see our heavenly Father. Someone who's always there, almost always smiling, always glad to see you, always glad to share a belly laugh. That father can be stern, but always in a loving way — never harsh, never cutting, never biting. Even when his kids know they've blown it, they don't feel scared to talk with him about it. He fosters a relationship where his children can tell him anything. Consequences may come, even punishment. But in the midst of all that, he would never speak to them out of condemnation. His children would feel comfortable and safe speaking to him, no matter what they had done.

Is that an easy relationship dynamic to master? Hardly. Every one of us, even the greatest of dads, falls short. But it's an ideal we should strive for every day. Fatherhood is about being engaged with your kids, talking with them, wrestling with them, holding them when they need to be held. It's wanting to be there for the first step and all the steps thereafter, not fleeing into the safety of a man cave or escaping to the security of work. Sure, career is important, but it's a short, flighty thing compared to your relationship with your kids. You may go through five or ten jobs during your working life. The relationship you have with your children lasts a lifetime. Or it should, and it will, if you connect with them emotionally when they're young.

Meeting the Challenge

Of course, being a "big tree" or a jolly, welcoming father doesn't sound all that heroic. And maybe to some, it doesn't even sound all that manly. Picking up a Ken doll and playing with your daughter and her Barbie Dreamhouse sounds, well, just about as unmanly as you can get. It's not much like extinguishing a fire that very well might burn down the entire Grand Canyon.

But to me, the willingness to grab that Ken doll and play with your daughter for a while lies at the heart of true manhood.

Look in the Bible and you'll find that love, the secret to fatherhood, often gets explicitly tied to the idea of sacrifice. "Love bears all things, believes all things, hopes all things, endures all things," Paul writes in 1 Corinthians 13:7 (ESV). In Romans 12:1 – 2, he writes, "I urge you, brothers and sisters, in view of God's mercy, to offer your bodies as a living sacrifice, holy and pleasing to God — this is your true and proper worship. Do not conform to the pattern of this world, but be transformed by the renewing of your mind. Then you will be able to test and approve what God's will is — his good, pleasing and perfect will."

The Lord wills that we be good fathers to our children and good husbands to our wives. Is manliness just brute power and strength and might? Or does it say, "I'm going to lay down my life for you"? On the surface, sacrifice can feel weak and powerless, but it's not. It's powerful. Christ may have looked weak and powerless on the cross during his moment of ultimate sacrifice, and yet that sacrifice remains the most powerful act the universe has ever seen.

It's another paradox. We are at our strongest when we lay down our lives, even in small ways, for our wives and children — maybe especially in small ways. It's hard to do. We get into arguments because we don't always do it well. But I guess that's why it's called a "sacrifice." If it were easy, it wouldn't be a sacrifice.

When you look at healthy families, you see one common characteristic — *sacrificial men*. Men who take time out for their kids — even when they'd rather do something else. Men who talk with their kids — even when some part of them just wants to watch the football game. Men who deal patiently with their kids — even when they've got to mop up the spilled milk from the floor for the third time that week. When men do the right thing for their families and offer that life-giving sacrifice, it pays big dividends. The families that result from that kind of fatherly commitment enjoy robust health.

After a recent broadcast for Focus on the Family, Karen Ehman, author of *Let. It. Go.: How to Stop Running the Show and Start Walking in Faith*, told a powerful story to our producer that had to do with her husband, Todd.

When their kids were younger, Todd worked as a youth pastor, which, as any youth pastor will tell you, is a full-time job, plus about thirty or fifty more hours. One day, just after he got home from rappelling with his junior high group and got ready to walk out the door to do another team outreach thing, Todd knelt in front of his daughter, who was about four at the time, and said, "Honey, I'm going to share Jesus with these teens, and I need your prayers."

"Oh good, Daddy!" his daughter said, quite sincerely. "When are you going to stay home and share Jesus with me?"

Todd left his ministry position, took a job at GM as a line assemblyman, and started getting home at five every day. He still does ministry, but he stayed home every night with his kids as they grew up. That's courageous fathering. I know it convicted me.

I'm not saying everyone should follow Todd's example. My own job sometimes requires travel and time away that I'd like to spend at home. It requires balance. But as fathers, we have to challenge ourselves to make sacrifices for our kids. We need to not only tell them that we love them but also show them that they're among the most important people in the world to us. That might sometimes lead us to make radical choices. But being a dad is, or at least it should be, a pretty radical experience.

When my stepfather walked out of our family's life forever, he told us he couldn't deal with it. That, to me, is the antithesis of fatherhood. God calls us as men to deal with discomforting situations such as the ones fatherhood can put us in. We're called to sacrifice for our families. We're called to be the men our wives and children need, and the heroes God wants us to be.

───────── **TO THINK ABOUT** ─────────

1. As a father, did you ever experience times when you felt like you couldn't deal with a situation anymore? Times when you wanted to run away? How did you get over those times?

2. Describe the most heroic thing you've ever done.

3. How have you sacrificed for your family? Are there areas in your life where you feel you should sacrifice more?

Three

Patching Holes

When I was eleven years old, my sister, Dee Dee, and I moved in with my biological dad — a second chance for us to become a real family.

The first time hadn't ended so well, crashing down all at once when I was five. It ended when I watched the police slap handcuffs on my father and lead him away, drunk and raging.

But six years is a long time when you're a kid, and we'd both been through a lot since then. I'd lost my mom. My stepfather had left us. My foster family fluctuated somewhere between a joke and a nightmare. With all that I'd been through, the chance to live with my dad again felt like, well, like coming home. It didn't matter to me that "home" amounted to a one-bedroom apartment in San Gabriel, California, furnished with white, plastic patio furniture and filled with the smell of cigarettes. I'd lived in much worse places. It didn't matter that some of my most vivid memories of my father reeked of moments of shame, confusion, and disappointment. He was Dad, *my* dad. He loved me, even if he didn't always know how to show it. In six years, I'd grown up a lot. And somewhere in my eleven-year-old mind, I believed that maybe he had too. Maybe he had gotten a better grasp on what a father was supposed to be.

It didn't take long to figure out that our "second chance" with Dad looked a lot like the first one.

He tried, I'll give him that. But he continued to drink, and I hated to be around him when he drank. And that meant I hardly came home. So I'd play sports — basketball or baseball or football or whatever sport the season called for. On Saturdays I'd play baseball all day. The kids who typically played ball in the morning came and left, and then the afternoon group came and left. I'd play with them both, maybe taking a break just to run home and make a sandwich or something. And because a kid like me can't play enough baseball, I got involved in the San Gabriel Little League too.

Maybe I got my love of baseball from my father. As a huge fan, he played quite a bit himself in his younger days. When Mike and Dave came along, he connected with them through baseball — teaching them to hit, playing catch with them, the whole works. He even coached their Little League teams. He got so involved with them that my brothers actually got annoyed with him for getting too involved.

I never had to deal with that problem. I can't remember my dad ever coaching me or ever giving me a tip on how to hit better. We rarely even played catch.

But he did come to watch one of my Little League games one day. He came drunk.

It was obvious to me, to the kids, to parents — to everyone. The moment the game started, he began slurring and muttering to himself, almost like the town drunks you'd see in old Westerns. I could hear him from the bench — that familiar intoxicated drawl of his — as parents around him leaned away and my teammates snickered.

And then came my turn to bat. I stepped into the batter's box and heard, behind me, that familiar drunken voice: "Thasss ma boy!"

I wish I wasn't here, I remember thinking as I stepped into the box. *I want to get out of here.* But I couldn't go anywhere. In that moment, standing to the side of home plate, I became the most visible person on the field, just when I wanted to become invisible. I felt desperate to get away, to hide from the humiliation, the shame.

"Thasss ma boy!" he had said. Everyone now knew my secret. Everyone would know forever.

The ball whipped past and thudded into the catcher's glove behind me. "Strike one!" the umpire bellowed.

"Waaddyre mean?!" my father hollered. "Yer crazy! Yer can't see anythin'!"

My mind raced. *Why is he acting like this?* I thought. Remember, I'm only in sixth grade, desperately trying to be normal. I just wanted to be an okay kid with an okay family. *Why is my dad acting like such an ass?*

"Strike two!" the ump said as another fastball whistled past.

"Ump, yer crazy!" I heard my father holler. I couldn't bear to look at him, but I imagined him nearly falling over in his drunken incredulity. *It figures. One of the few times my dad shows an interest in my baseball, and he shows up drunk.* I couldn't concentrate on the pitches. Fastball after fastball whizzed by, and I couldn't concentrate. What hope did I have of catching up with one of those things? How could I try to make my dad proud when I didn't want him there at all?

"Strike three!"

I didn't talk with my dad after the game. I cold-shouldered him. And really, what was there to say? Both of us had struck out.

Barriers

As we talk about what it means to be a great father, we have to acknowledge that some very real obstacles can block our path, among them barriers of our own making — sins, weaknesses, and addictions that undercut our ability to be fully there for our kids. Sometimes we had no part in creating these blockades, but still we must find a way to overcome them. Whether or not they're our fault, these things can overwhelm us and destroy our ability to be the fathers God meant for us to be.

My own dad provides a sobering example of such destructive power in action. By the time I came back into his life at age eleven, he had all but checked out. I believe the level of regret in his life had topped out, and as much as he wanted to be a good father, he just couldn't figure out how to do it. His sense of failure overwhelmed him. His demons were just too strong for him.

We slept in the same bedroom the year I lived with him, in a tiny apartment where my sister slept on the couch in the living room. She didn't stick around much, though. I remember waking up many times in the middle of the night — two, three in the morning — and finding Dad not in bed with me.

I'd walk out of the bedroom, turn a corner, and look into the living room. And I'd see the ashy-orange glow of a cigarette in the gloom — turning brighter when Dad inhaled, tiny pinpricks of light floating for an instant as he tapped the cigarette into an unseen ashtray.

The rest of the apartment remained pitch-dark. The only light came from the glow of the cigarette. I don't know how long I watched him smoke — a couple of minutes at most, maybe. But it seemed, sometimes, like hours — the glow of the cigarette tip growing brighter and fainter; the slow, steady breathing of my dad; the flyaway ashes dancing above the ash-tray for an instant before blinking into nothing.

It was quite a moment for an eleven-year-old to stare across that black living room and see only that glow. *What's he doing there?* I wondered. *What's he thinking?* Looking back, I can imagine what was going through his mind — worry. He was almost seventy, still doing manual labor as a furniture manu-facturer. And now, he had a little boy in his life who, somehow, he needed to raise to manhood. How could he do it? I'll bet his thoughts ran along the lines of, *What am I going to do?* He was old and tired and plagued by some very bad habits. He knew he couldn't be a good father if he drank all the time. But he never truly stopped. He always went back to the bottle. He *always* went back.

Vice and Addiction

By that time, my father had become a broken person, a guy who wanted to do the right thing but who couldn't find the will to do it, even at the cost of his family. I find it hard, even now, to really wrap my brain around that. It just grates against my senses. I can't imagine giving my kids up for alcohol — trading them in for another drink. That may sound very compassion-less to say, but I struggle with the idea of loving alcohol more than my kids.

Most addicts would probably argue with that character-ization. They might even say they love their children more than anything, way more than the next beer or next hit or next encounter with porn. And I believe it. But fatherhood, as we've noted, isn't just about *telling* your children you love them, but it's about *showing* them. And how do people plagued with addiction show their love? What sacrifices do they make?

What kind of commitment do they demonstrate to put away their vices for good to truly love and embrace the people whom they say matter the most? It discourages me to see how many can't or won't.

I think some men struggle not so much with clinical addiction as with the desire to hang on to adolescence. It gets back to the old cliché of kids having kids. And while marriage and parenthood *can* provide a trigger into a greater sense of maturity — the tilt of the box I mentioned in chapter 2 — some men resist that tilt with all their might, clinging by their fingernails so they won't slide into God's side of the box. You find people in their thirties who'd rather play video games and drink beer with their buddies than become *real* husbands and fathers. Lack of maturity is a huge and growing problem.

Then you have people who have a literal addiction to something. The addiction itself keeps them from growing. It arrests their development, and they become, at least with regard to their addiction, almost like infants. They *need* it. They have to have it. And if the addiction grows strong enough, they'll do almost anything to get it. The long-term benefits of a relationship with their kids become secondary to getting some relief from that in-the-moment craving.

The two problems, obviously, often go together. Immaturity leads to an addiction. And addiction will almost always make men act incredibly immature.

But both represent the same core problem — an unwillingness to listen to what God has in store for their life. An unwillingness to make the right, but difficult, choices. An inclination to fill the holes in a life with the worst sorts of substances and images and vices possible, when the only thing capable of really filling those cavities is God. And the act of filling those cavities — the desire to patch that hole and the shame we use as filler — can make the problem grow worse.

Lorraine Pintus, author of *Jump Off the Hormone Swing*, appeared on the Focus on the Family Daily Broadcast in 2013 to discuss menopause and premenstrual syndrome. I know, I know. Right up my alley, right? Anyway, she spoke about body chemistry and how when she felt a PMS moment coming on, she had a huge craving for chocolate and ice cream. Once she satisfied her craving by eating a chocolate bar or a dish of ice cream or something, she felt some relief — for about five minutes. After that, she'd crash again, only this time much worse.

When she looked into the science of these episodes — the body chemistry behind both her monthly cycles and her cravings — she discovered that the chocolate and ice cream might help in the short term, but chemically they actually made things worse. What an irony, she said, that the very thing that temporarily made her feel good also took her body even lower.

I think we deal with a similar cycle when it comes to issues of addiction. An alcoholic man may feel horrible about the way he acts when he's drunk, or about the drinking itself. He may feel miserable that it's come between him and his family, or that it keeps him from being the man he wants to be. But fixing the problem seems so daunting, almost impossible. So what does he do? He turns to the very thing that's making him miserable and finds a temporary escape there. But in that escape, he builds his own shame and regret.

What are we trying to fill with these vices of ours? From what are we trying to run away? We turn to these addictions, whether it's pornography or drinking or drugs or anything else, for countless reasons. But maybe the number one reason points right back to what we discussed in chapter 1 — the fact that we often feel out of control or don't feel competent in who we are as men. We feel overwhelmed by our own insecurities and brokenness. And so we run away from our own failures.

I know of a man going through this stuff right now. He has a wonderful, sweet wife and a beautiful, little five-year-old girl. But alcohol clouds his priorities. And each time he gets drunk, his home life gets a little worse. He drives another wedge between himself and the members of his family. He loves his family, he says, but that might not help him keep them. He could lose everything because he has refused to master these vices of his. It just shows us their blinding power.

I wish I could say these things had an easy fix. Just flip the right switch or go to the right seminar or pray the exact right prayer, and the addictions vanish. But any expert in addiction will tell you that's just not so. I saw this myself as I watched my dad — a man I loved and a man who loved me — who couldn't break away from his demons. So in the end I had to break away from him.

Man's Troubles, God's Timing

I didn't know it at the time, but my still-drinking dad had become suicidal. Dee learned that he spent one afternoon sitting in a park and holding a razor blade, struggling with whether to slash his wrists. He eventually decided to live and come home, but his thoughts grew increasingly darker — which meant he probably wasn't the best person to trust to raise a kid.

Dee was turning eighteen and about to leave the apartment for good. I was about to turn twelve, and my brothers and sisters were afraid to leave me in that environment. They never told me about my father's suicidal thoughts. They merely said

I needed to move out — and that I needed to be the one to tell my father. He wouldn't accept it from anyone else.

And so I did. It was hard, but I did it. I had to look my father in the eye and tell him, "I don't think I should live with you anymore."

When I said that, he looked stunned, like I had just hit him with a two-by-four. "Why?" he asked.

"Because of the way you treated Mom," I blurted. I couldn't think of anything else to say.

And to his credit, he stood up and hugged me. "You know, I haven't been a good husband, and I'm not a good father." He hugged me again and left.

He died four months later. They found his frozen body in an abandoned building in Reno, Nevada. He'd been drinking, of course. He drank so much that he passed out, I guess, and never woke up. To this day, it's still hard to think of him like that.

Addictions are awful, no question. They can destroy families and kill people. But even so, there's hope too. We know these addictions can be conquered. We've all seen it happen.

When my nephew struggled with his own addiction to alcohol, my oldest brother, Mike, did his best to help him. He invited my sister's son to live with him, but under some pretty tight restrictions — all that "tough love" stuff you hear about. Obviously, he couldn't touch a drop of alcohol while he lived with his uncle. If he did, Mike told him, he'd have to evict him. Sometimes, such strong measures are just what an addict needs to keep him or her on the right path. And Mike had determined to help his nephew conquer his problems.

But dealing with addiction is never easy. Counselors will tell you it's a lifelong battle, and many addicts stumble on the way to real recovery. It probably shouldn't have surprised anyone that this alcoholic started sneaking drinks up to his room. When Mike caught him, he had to kick him out. After living with Mike for three or four months, the guy found himself out on the street. It must've been tremendously difficult.

But Mike never gave up on his nephew, even when forced to evict him. They would continue to see each other often and pray together. They kept doing a Bible study together. Rules are rules that must be enforced, but even when they get broken, love doesn't have to go away.

And then, a little miracle happened. The addict had an encounter with the Lord. That became the turning point. Once he found Christ, he got the help he needed, and today he's in a much better place. I'm proud of him for waking up and getting through each day without a drink.

The sad truth is that we men often turn to things that destroy us — more, I think, than women do. It's a pattern in us. We can see it in our addictions. We can see it in our attraction to gangs. We feel drawn to violence. We gravitate toward sex and substances. We try to pull fulfillment or escape from these things, when we know deep in our souls that they can't "fix" us. They can't mend the holes in our hearts.

So how do we deal with that? How do we fix it? I think we have to get to the place where my nephew ended up — to a place where we can truly accept the help offered to us. I don't know if anyone can give advice to someone in the throes of addiction unless that person's heart has grown ready to receive it and act on it. I saw that with this young man, who, after much trial and error, finally got the help he needed.

Overcoming addiction takes someone who is willing to reach out, like my brother did. But it also takes someone willing to grab hold of that outstretched hand. You can't *force* an addict to get better. You can't make him do the right thing.

He has to want to deal with the addiction. He has to deal with whatever holes he's trying to patch with the addiction. And if he's a father, he has to walk the walk. If he loves his family more than his habit, he has to prove it, first to himself and then to them.

The Dad-Shaped Hole

As men, we can come to the table of fatherhood pretty messed up. We may be dealing with these cavities in our souls that we try to patch with all sorts of impotent remedies. But sometimes these holes don't form as the products of vice or addiction. Maybe we don't have a big issue with drinking or porn or the other common temptations that bedevil so many men, but many of us deal with another huge problem, one I'm personally and deeply cognizant of. We have a hole left behind by our own fathers. A father who hurt us. A father who ignored us. A father we never knew.

I didn't have opportunity to learn much from the "fathers" in my life. And I know I'm not alone. Many men labor at trying to figure out what it means to be a father because they've never had dads themselves. No wonder so many men walk into fatherhood scared. No wonder we feel intimidated by the job ahead of us. If we have no one around who can show us the ropes, how do we know what to do? Are we at greater risk for repeating the same mistakes our own dads made? How do we patch up *that* gaping hole?

Here's a hard truth: That hole is never going to be completely filled. You do like I did — you learn to live with it. But you always feel that absence in your soul. Nothing can ever make it completely better. But pragmatically, when we're talking about ways to overcome at least some of that hole and become a good father, the father you may never have had, there are ways to compensate. And one of the best is to find people in your life who can give you an inkling of what a good dad should look like.

A Life of Service

For nearly forty years, Paul Moro has coached high school football. He coached me when I played quarterback in Yucca Valley. These days, he leads the Blue Ridge High School Yellow Jackets. His teams have won twelve state championships, and he's just the third football coach in Arizona history to win more than three hundred games. He's a proven winner, but as a coach he's much more than that. He's able to take a team and make it into a sort of family. He really cares about the kids he coaches.

"What he did more than anything was develop a team atmosphere that resonated so deep inside of you that you were willing to do anything for him and your teammates," former Yellow Jacket Jeremy Hathcock told MaxPreps.com.[16] And even though he's in his early sixties now, Coach Moro still has the same attitude. I talked with him recently, just as he prepared to take a group of about a hundred high schoolers — from a public school, mind you — to Colorado for fun, honest discussion, and probably some tears. And yes, tough questions about attitude and God.

"How do you get away with that in public schools?" I asked him.

"It's what I do," he said. "They'd have to fire me if I couldn't do it. Life to me is service. And I've chosen to serve teenagers."

Life to me is service. That's profound. I'm not even sure if Paul understands how powerful that is, because he approaches things in such a simple, straightforward manner. But he gets it. He understands in a way that most men, even fathers who should be committed to a life of service to their wives and children, just don't.

You could see that sense of service in almost every afternoon drill, every pep talk. I think Coach Moro was trying to make men of us freshmen and sophomores — real men, greater men. I remember one afternoon in particularly vivid detail. We were in the middle of practice. As a freshman/sophomore, I played quarterback/free safety, pretty wet behind the ears. We had run a bunch of drills and wind sprints, and I must've just been going through the motions, jogging through the wind sprints — that kind of thing.

Coach Moro came right up to me and did something he'd probably not be able to get away with today: He grabbed me by the face mask, yanked my face close to his, and glared right into my eyes.

"Listen, if you're going to be the quarterback of this team before long," he said, "you gotta *lead* it. You've gotta finish your wind sprints *first*. Set the example."

It wasn't enough to throw the football seventy yards downfield. I had to work harder, show more hustle, give more effort, than anyone else. I had to show the rest of my team what being a part of this team meant, and what it took. Coach Moro wanted to get me to try harder. That year, I ended up playing defense and backup quarterback.

It was no big deal to him, maybe — a conversation he'd have with a handful of the players. But for me, it was a watershed moment. For me, it wasn't a question of being lazy. But I also didn't feel like I had what it took. I didn't have my head in the game. I had all the physical capabilities, but I couldn't rise above what was churning inside of me. And maybe all those insecurities kept me from giving it my all. Maybe, like so many of us, I was running away from my challenges. I didn't give it my all so I'd have a ready-made excuse if I failed.

Coach Moro could see all that. He knew I had the physical talent, but also that much inside of me handicapped me from becoming the leader I needed to be. In a way, maybe, I was still that boy playing Little League baseball, embarrassed and unsure and unable to swing the bat at the critical moment. I felt trapped in those old insecurities that had grown out of my experiences with my father and others. Coach Moro challenged me to get over it, to push past whatever got in my way and to work. To strive to be better, whether as a quarterback or a leader or a successful human being.

A lot of fathers could use someone like Paul Moro, someone who will grab their face masks and tell them to get their heads in the game.

But Coach Moro could see something else missing in me too. And he managed to help take care of that as well.

When I was a freshman, Coach Moro took several of my teammates and me to a Fellowship of Christian Athletes camp. One of the messages hit me hard, harder than anyone had ever hit me before, on or off the field. (Even harder than Glen smacking me in the sternum during PE class and making me feel far from being a man.)

The guy up in front started talking about fathers. "Has your father let you down?" he said. *Yes*, I thought. "Has your stepfather let you down?" *Yes*. My eyes opened wider. It felt eerie. I half expected the speaker to start detailing all the pain I'd experienced in my life at the hands of my father and would-be fathers: The drunken inconsistency, the cold indifference, the insanity of it all. It felt as though God had zeroed in right on me. And before I knew it, I had gone up front, tears pooling in my eyes, saying, "Yeah, I want to give my life to Christ."

I'm not sure how much we realize the kind of impact we can have on other people's lives by what we say and how we act. Coach Moro showed a compassion for me and an interest in me and my future that I'd never seen from my real fathers. And in that moment, just like my nephew when he stayed with my brother, my heart felt ready to receive some good advice. And so I received the Lord.

A Life of Integrity

Jeff Eves came into my life a little later, when he hired me out of college to work for Tension Envelope. We grew to become good friends, and he became a strong mentor in my life.

In some respects, he and Coach Moro had a lot in common. Coach would tell me that I needed to run my butt off if I was going to lead. Jeff would say, "If you're going to grow into something with this company, you have to go *this* way." Or, "If you want to go farther here, you'll need to do *this* better." He really took an interest in me, and it's no stretch to say he became something of a father figure to me. Nothing contrived about it, nothing forced. His mentorship came in a very natural way. Jeff rooted for me. He wanted me to succeed. And he would talk straight with me to help me achieve that success, just as any good father would. But perhaps the thing that impressed me the most about Jeff was his personal integrity.

A year or two into my career at Tension, I opened a sales office for Jeff in San Diego. He came down to see how things were going and ran a few of his personal bills through our postage machine in the office.

"How much do I owe you?" he asked.

"Probably a buck," I said. "Don't worry about it." But he wouldn't let it go. He insisted on paying. So, after a little back-and-forth, I agreed to add up the postage and found out that he owed the company a whopping $1.30. He fished in his pocket and handed me a dollar bill and three dimes.

"When the company hired me, they didn't agree to pay my postage," he said.

I know that sounds like a little thing. But maybe that's why it made such an incredible impression on me: *It was such a little thing.* In that moment, Jeff Eves taught me volumes about what it meant to be a person of integrity — you take care of the little things.

Going It Alone

You're wise to look for a role model. But before anyone starts casting around for some perfect guy to emulate, let me offer one caution. Role models are hard to find. And even if you find one, they're never perfect.

Both Coach Moro and Jeff Eves helped me to become the person I am today. I learned a lot from them, even lessons they might not have been aware of teaching. But while they taught me and served as role models for me, they never took the place of a father. They weren't there for me every day, as a father would've been. And while they taught me to be a better *man*, I didn't learn how to be a better *father* from either of them.

I learned what a father looks like by looking at my own "fathers" and seeing they didn't look much like fathers at all. In seeing what my own father figures lacked, I saw more clearly what a real father should be — or at least what I desperately wanted a father to be. My dad wasn't around much, so I knew a dad should be present. He was erratic, so I knew a dad should be constant and reliable. My stepfather was all about rules and punishment, so I longed for love and acceptance. Even though I never had a good dad, my experience with not-so-good dads helped forge the way ahead.

Think about what you missed out on because of your father, or what you missed *in* your father. Think of those times when your dad wounded you or made it more difficult for you as a child, as a teen, as a young adult. Write those things out, literally, on a piece of paper. If that feels a little weird, just write them out in your mind, like I did. Did your father abuse you? Was he never home? When did he make you feel small? Insignificant? Then look at what you've written (either on that sheet of paper or in your mind) and say, "These are the things I don't ever want to do as a father."

From there, you probably won't find it too hard to see what a good father, a father like you, should do. And as you formulate that list, you might find you already have a pretty good role model after all.

Our Father, Who Art in Heaven

The Bible so often refers to the Lord as "Father" that we sometimes forget how significant that word really is with regard to describing the nature of God. We understand that God is the Father of all creation, "from whom all things came and for whom we live" (1 Corinthians 8:6). We understand that he's Jesus' Father, of course. But we forget that God explicitly asks *us* to call him Father. Through both him and his Son, we can get a pretty good glimpse at what we as earthbound dads should look like.

"Don't you know me, Philip, even after I have been among you such a long time?" Jesus asks in John 14:9. Then Jesus goes on to say, "Anyone who has seen me has seen the Father. How can you say, 'Show us the Father'?"

So what sort of Father do we see? In many respects, we see the sort of dad I longed for throughout my childhood, the image of a father by which everyone else in my life fell woefully short.

He loves us more deeply, more powerfully than we can imagine; and he showed us that love through sacrifice: "But because of his great love for us, God, who is rich in mercy, made us alive with Christ even when we were dead in transgressions — it is by grace you have been saved" (Ephesians 2:4 – 5).

He remains utterly dependable in his character and in his affection for us: "Because of the LORD's great love we are not consumed, for his compassions never fail. They are new every morning; great is your faithfulness" (Lamentations 3:22 – 23). He's always with us.

> Where can I go from your Spirit?
>> Where can I flee from your presence?
> If I go up to the heavens, you are there;
>> if I make my bed in the depths, you are there.
> If I rise on the wings of the dawn,
>> if I settle on the far side of the sea,
> even there your hand will guide me,
>> your right hand will hold me fast.
>
> Psalm 139:7 – 10

When I consider those attributes of God, they make him sound, in a way, like that strong oak, that jolly father, discussed in the last chapter. God really *is* a great example of what a father should be. And if our own fathers failed us, we shouldn't let those failures obscure the model of our ultimate Abba Father.

One of the hardest times of my life happened just a few years ago when I became the president of Focus on the Family. I was replacing Dr. James Dobson, one of the most prophetic and respected Christian leaders of the twentieth century.

All leadership transitions are filled with challenges, but replacing a man like Dr. Dobson is particularly daunting. After all, he built Focus from the ground up, and for more than thirty years, "Doctor," as we called him, was the face, the voice, and the mind behind the ministry. When he decided the time had come to step down and start preparing the way for new leadership, we all knew we faced a hard road ahead. And when he tapped me as his successor, I knew I faced a huge challenge.

It turned out to be even harder than I thought.

It didn't help that my transition coincided with a terrible economic downturn, which saw Focus's financial support shrink. Add to that the fact that my leadership style differs greatly from that of Dr. Dobson, that I have different strengths and weaknesses and don't sound the same on the radio. Let's face it — change is hard. People said inaccurate and hurtful things, and I had no way to defend myself. (And nothing I said would have made much of a difference anyway.)

In the midst of all that transition pain, old insecurities started creeping in again. Old wounds from my youth started to ache. In some respects, it felt like I was reliving my childhood.

One morning as I found myself in the middle of all this, I thought of Dr. Dobson and envied the wonderful family he had while growing up. He had often talked about how much he learned from his mom and dad. He'd go hunting with his father and gained so much wisdom from him. And later, when Doc really needed to hash out a tricky issue in the early days of Focus, he'd ask his father for advice. He always had a father to lean on.

I recalled my conversations with Dr. Dobson, remembering how much he'd loved, revered, and relied on his father. I thought about the maelstrom that surrounded me. To put it bluntly, I threw a big pity party for myself. *If only I had a dad,* I thought. *Doc had a dad he could call. Doc had someone to ask what to do.*

And then I heard something, deep in my heart. "Haven't I been a good Father to you?"

If you're not a Christian, that's a hard thing to grasp. But the thought, the voice, came out of nowhere. I hadn't been looking for encouragement or a rebuke. But it came, unbidden, wafting through my soul like a breeze. It even had tone to it.

In an instant, I remembered all the moments in my life that today seem like miracles. How I almost miraculously was given the ability to push through some horrifically painful moments. How God brought people into my life at just the right times. How he guided my shaking steps through the weeks and months and years. How he somehow brought me — that scared, insecure kid who struck out while his drunken father bellowed from the stands — to a place where I could help tens of thousands of other families. How he gave me a family of my own.

Haven't I been a good Father to you?

I fell to my knees and put my face to the ground. "You've been an awesome Dad," I said. "Thank you."

A friend of mine told me of walking along the shores of Galilee a couple of summers ago. He saw a little boy, maybe five or six years old, walking behind his father, picking up seashells. And then, suddenly, the boy found something amazing in the sand. Something wonderful.

"Abba!" he cried out, running toward his father with a huge smile on his face. "Abba!"

Paul writes, "The Spirit we received brought about your adoption to sonship. And by him we cry, '*Abba*, Father'" (Romans 8:15).

We're to call him *Abba*. Father. Daddy. He loves us. He cares for us. And unlike our real fathers sometimes do, he will never *ever* leave us.

He is an awesome Father.

────────────── **TO THINK ABOUT** ──────────────

1. Are you dealing with addictions or distractions that make it difficult to be the dad you know you need to be?

2. When you think of your own father, what did he do right? What did he do wrong? What did your father do, either good or bad, that can teach you a valuable lesson?

3. Are there men in your life who make excellent role models for being a good dad? Who are they? What lessons can they teach you? Have you ever talked to them about these strong points you see in them?

Four

Nobody's Perfect

IF I EVER WRITE A NO-NONSENSE, BY-THE-NUMBERS RULE book on parenting, lesson no. 1,178 will be as follows: Never leave a pair of jumper cables unattended on the kitchen counter (no matter how small the jumper cables may be).

For some fathers, this might just be common sense. Not for me.

A few years ago, Jean bought a couple of science kits at Hobby Lobby (on sale for $14.99) for Trent, Troy, and me to play with. One of them was designed to extract hydrogen gas — essentially rocket fuel — from the atmosphere. I won't bore you with the details, but it involved a battery, a couple of test tubes, a tiny set of jumper cables, and, if you *really* want to impress your nine-year-old and seven-year-old boys, a match. (Just do the experiment, light the hydrogen gas in the test tube, and watch it go BOOM! And then listen to your boys say, "You're the coolest dad *ever!*")

The boys and I had a great time doing the experiment. What fun when you can safely trigger explosions in your own kitchen! Trent, our oldest, particularly enjoyed it. He has a keen scientific mind, much like his mom, and seeing how things work has always fascinated him. Ever since he learned to talk, he's asked questions about the world around him.

Naturally, Troy loves to do everything Trent loves to do, and as a dad, I enjoy taking part in my sons' scientific adventures. I absolutely love watching them discover new things and expand their imaginations. To see the world through his children's eyes is one of the greatest joys a dad can have. You can experience the wonder of God's creation, almost as if for the first time.

But as much as we would've loved to play with the science kits for the rest of that evening, we couldn't. Jean and I had to go to a dinner engagement — Colorado Springs' annual Christian-Jewish Dialogue dinner, not exactly a hot ticket for children. So eventually I got up, got ready, gave the babysitter some last-minute instructions, gave the boys hugs, and walked out the door.

I left the jumper cables on the kitchen counter. In the same house with two adventurous, scientifically inclined boys.

You might as well leave Wile E. Coyote with a package of dynamite.

Right in the middle of the dinner's "dialogue" portion of the festivities, with speakers discussing and debating religious issues of the day, we heard Jean's phone buzz in her purse. Obviously, we weren't going to answer it at the table with the presentations going on. So we snuck out of the banquet area and into the hallway, where we could listen to the message.

Every parent, I think, understands the sharp pang of fear when they receive an unexpected message from home. Your head may tell you everything's fine, but deep down, you worry. Somewhere deep in the most illogical recesses of your brain, you conjure up images of fire and floods and burglars. Maybe an invasion of Huns.

Jean quickly dialed in to hear the message, both of us hoping everything was all right.

"Hi, Mommy," chirped Troy's voice. "Trenton actually was dumb enough to get the battery that I licked with my tongue on the mini jump cables — and actually plug it in the DVD player, and it caused smoke! But don't worry ... it did not start a fire. This is Troy, and by the way, Trent did it — okay? Okay. Have I been specific enough? Okay, bye!"

There was more. Drawing out his words as if to amplify the effect, Troy — acting like our very own Dennis the Menace — added the following with the sort of glee only a younger brother can muster when he's got something on his older bro: "Oh, besides, don't ... go ... easy ... on ... Trent!"

We didn't know precisely what that message meant, something about smoke and Troy's tongue and perhaps a damaged DVD player. But all things considered, we felt pretty relieved. From the sound of things, the boys remained safe (though one of them might still have smoke curling off of his tongue). We had no burglars outside the window, no Huns circling the property. The house, despite Trent's efforts to the contrary, had not burned down (though I have to admit that when we got home, I was happy to see no fire trucks parked in the driveway). We felt less concerned about our boys, in fact, than where our favorite babysitter had been during this whole saga. It seemed like she was totally out of the picture, doing homework or on the phone or something. Yikes!

But we knew we'd be able to sort out the whole thing once we got home. Jean and I had a good laugh, offered our regrets to our hosts, and left.

But the events of the evening weren't nearly as funny for Trent. While Jean and I laughed, Troy acted as the Daly family's own prophet of doom.

"You're gonna be in *big* trouble," Troy would be saying. "Dad's gonna *kill* you when he gets home." I expect every time Trent looked at him, Troy would ominously drag his index finger across his neck, like a pint-size mafioso — a subtle sign of what awaited poor Trent.

When we arrived home, it took us twenty minutes to find Trent. We finally located him, hiding in a shelf in Troy's room, maybe hoping he could hide there until the time came for him to go to college. It took me another twenty-five minutes to convince him that everything was okay. Really.

"You're not going to kill me?" he asked.

"No, of course not," I said. "You're a *scientist*. Scientists are supposed to experiment. Next time, though, don't experiment with electricity when I'm not around." I paused and then added, "or on your younger brother."

The Divided Soul

"If only there were evil people somewhere insidiously committing evil deeds, and it were necessary only to separate them from the rest of us and destroy them," wrote the great Russian writer Aleksandr Solzhenitsyn. "But the line dividing good and evil cuts through the heart of every human being."[17]

A concise, if ineloquent, paraphrase of Solzhenitsyn might be, *Nobody's perfect.*

We mean well (most of the time). We want to do what's right (when it's convenient). But sometimes we fall short. We make mistakes. We sin. And even though all of us know that nobody's perfect, it's interesting how often we forget it.

Some people expect that the head of Focus on the Family should have a perfect family. Maybe they think it's part of the job description: "Those with imperfect families need not apply." Sometimes people make the same assumptions about their pastors and their families, or their seemingly picture-perfect neighbors up the street. We look at what's on the outside, the sparkling veneers most of us try to show the world, and we assume it looks pretty and clean all the way through.

Stories like the one above — and many, many others — prove that my family, as much as I love it, isn't all *that* perfect. A perfect Trent wouldn't have stuck a jumper cable where it clearly shouldn't go. A perfect Troy would not have spent half the night scaring the stuffing out of poor Trent. And a perfect dad, one who knows full well his boys' penchant for experimentation, wouldn't have left those jumper cables out to begin with.

On some level, of course, we know it. We're quite aware of our own flaws and mistakes. And even if we're blind to them, someone will be sure to come along and tell us. For Christians, our own imperfections form a critical cornerstone for our faith. We're all sinners, we're told — all of us full of faults, failings, and imperfections. We can never be perfect, we're told — no matter how hard we try — and so God's grace and forgiveness alone can save us.

It's interesting that many of us, even as we read these words and repeat them in church and believe them with all our heart, still have a hard time accepting this as truth. Imperfections surround us, but we still treat them as if they're aberrations, almost insults to who and what we are. Even Christians, steeped in the idea that imperfection is a big part of what we are, have a hard time tolerating it in others. We parents, who should know full well all the mistakes *we* made as children, don't always show a lot of grace and forgiveness to our own kids. We fathers can forget that our children are fallible. We can forget that we can't be perfect either — and either we believe we are perfect (or close to it), and thus deny reality, or we're so aware of our imperfections that we have a hard time accepting them and accepting ourselves in the midst of them. Despite the fact that Jesus modeled grace and forgiveness, we have a hard time giving that same sort of grace and forgiveness to others. We end up lying to ourselves. We end up pretending before God. How contrary to who God is and what he expects of us!

Bono, lead singer for U2, had an interesting take on this when I interviewed him in 2013. He told me, "God is much more interested in who you are than who you want to be."

The Quest for Perfection

When I think about our desire to be perfect, I think about David, God's anointed king of Israel and a deeply flawed man. When we look at the political scandals of today, not many hold a candle to David's.

Outwardly, Israel's second king looked like a pretty perfect guy. He was a fantastic leader, a great poet, and beloved by God. He protected his kingdom, expanded its borders, and regularly showed mercy and kindness in an age not known for much of either.

But as we know, David wasn't nearly as perfect as people thought he was, or as perfect as he pretended to be. He slept with a married woman named Bathsheba and, to keep his sin a secret, sent the woman's husband into the thick of battle to his death — adultery and murder, plain and simple. And for a while, David thought he had gotten away with it.

But one day, the prophet Nathan visited the palace and confronted David with his evil behavior. And David learned that while he might've been able to keep secrets from his whole kingdom, he couldn't hide sin from God. The Lord caught him and punished him.

But David *repented* of his sin. He ran out of control at times, totally unbridled, unhinged from conviction. But eventually he acknowledged his wrongdoing and mistakes. He didn't quit or give up. He learned from his actions and went right back to a better path, making amends along the way. God forgave him. And God never stopped loving him.

That doesn't mean David dodged the consequences. Though God punished him, he didn't end their relationship.

I hope most of us won't need to be forgiven of murder. But just as David learned from his own failures, so we can draw lessons from those failures. If David — blessed by God with great ability, loved like crazy, and anointed as the leader of God's chosen people — can so badly mess up, then what hope do the rest of us have?

David's sin didn't shock God. He knew the guy better than David knew himself. God understands the capacity we have for sin and temptation, and while that might grieve him, it doesn't surprise him. David was bound to fail at something. We're all bound to stumble and fall. Nothing we do will ever leave God bewildered, saying, "Well, I never thought he'd do *that*."

That doesn't mean God *accepts* our sin, but merely that he acknowledges the reality that we *will* sin. He made us, so he understands our imperfections better than we do ourselves. And because he's God, he can often use the thing that most drives us apart as a tool to bring us closer together. He uses our own weaknesses to bring about an experience of a greater and deeper relationship.

Think of it as a little like a father's bond with his kids. The smaller and weaker our children, the more they depend on us as dads for care and protection and guidance. Their weakness brings father and child closer. And God longs for that close-ness with us. Sometimes we might pretend we don't need God. But we do. We always do and always will. We're small and weak. When we admit that, it allows the Lord to draw closer to us. And we're at our weakest when we show the world (or even ourselves) just how imperfect we are.

The comparison becomes easy to see when we think in terms of physical weakness. As dads, we know we have to protect and guide our five-year-olds. They need us. But the metaphor strains for some of us when we exchange the idea of physical weakness for an emotional, mental, or spiritual sense of underdevelopment — what we might call *mistakes*. Sometimes these mistakes can be purposeful and harmful. Sometimes they can be unintentional, the product of not yet knowing the rules. But as a dad, the distinction doesn't always matter. When our kids spill grape juice on the carpet or scrawl pictures all over the kitchen cabinets or hit their little sisters for no reason, we don't feel so big or protective. If your daughter puts a dent in your car or your son sets fire to the garage, those don't feel like opportunities to bond. And if we catch our kids in something sinful or unlawful — lying, stealing, drinking — those things drive wedges between us more often than they bring us closer together.

I think Christians may have a harder time dealing with mistakes than nonbelievers. Some of my friends who aren't Christians have tremendous relationships with their kids. They have a great rapport with them, in part because they have a basic acceptance of their humanity, an understanding of their own innate weaknesses. That seems easier for nonbelievers to accept. As Christians, we have very high standards for our kids, and perhaps rightly so. But that can also make us more intolerant of mistakes than we should be. We live in a state of constantly trying to become more perfect — again, a good thing, but a striving that can lead to some very bad things. When we aim for perfection, an inherently impossible standard to reach, we run the danger of not just encouraging our children to do better and to improve but of telling them they're just not good enough and they will *never* be good enough.

But that's a *me* problem, not a *God* problem. When you look at it from God's point of view, I doubt he's looking for perfection, since he knows it's impossible for us to attain. He's looking instead for a continuously better relationship with him. Sometimes the moments we veer off course are the exact moments we swerve closer to our Lord. Sometimes when we feel as though God is grading us with an F, we're actually getting an A. Why? Because we're getting closer to the One who made us and realizing our dependence on him. We're depending on the payment of perfection that Jesus provided by dying for each of us.

Learning Lessons

This doesn't mean God likes us to make mistakes or commit sins. He simply knows that we will and expects us to learn from them and not repeat those mistakes. So how do we turn our mistakes into lessons? How do we teach our kids how to deal with mistakes correctly, not by flogging themselves over them, not by accepting them like they're no big deal, but by growing from them?

In my family, it begins with a talk. I regularly talk to my boys about how none of us are perfect, me included. If you were to ask my kids what I tell them about perfection, they'd say, "Oh, he says he's not perfect. And we're not perfect." I've tried to plant that thought in their minds — that we're all works in progress in God's eyes.

There's a big difference between "not good enough" and "not perfect." When you're talking about perfection, you're talking about God's standard of measure. To understand that we're not perfect, and can never be perfect in God's eyes, develops in us a healthy understanding of reality — God's reality. We *all* fall short of God's standard of perfection.

From there, we build in the theology of the acceptance of Christ and sanctification and trying by his power to do better. We can teach our kids that, when we fail, we must turn to God and ask for forgiveness, just as David did. And by extension, doing this will help us teach how important it is to apologize to the people in our lives whom we've hurt through our mistakes and shortcomings.

This understanding of our own imperfections helps us avoid the modern-day legalism that endangers so many Christians. We in the Christian community need to learn to relax a little, to realize that perfection for our kids remains out of reach. Sure, we want them to learn and grow from their mistakes all the time; we will help them see that God wants us to live every day in a way that shows we are making progress. But we have to understand, and help our kids understand, that we all fail sometimes. And that failure is okay.

Let me repeat that: It's okay for your kids to fail sometimes. Because that's often how they learn the best.

It's a tough balancing act, but it's a challenge that all dads deal with at some point — and may even have opportunities to teach several times a day.

I just had a moment like this with Trent not too long ago. He lied to me about finishing his math homework. When I discovered the truth, I sat him down for a talk. We talked about why it's important to work hard in school. We talked about why lying, particularly to your father, is never appropriate. We talked about how we're made in God's image and how we need to strive to be more like Jesus every day.

I wanted to turn his mistake into an opportunity to learn and grow — not to make him feel like a failure (because he had failed) but to help him understand why it's important to do better the next time.

Own Up

It took time to get to this point, to understand that mistakes are just lessons in disguise. My frustration level when my boys were younger rose much higher than it does today. I can feel myself mellowing out. And I'm happy with that. I like it.

For me, it's all about concentrating on the things I should concentrate on. The things I can teach. The love I can show. The ability, when something bad happens, to put my arm around my child and say, "It'll be okay."

That's so important, because kids have such great fears about disappointing us or letting us down. They worry about consequences. And honestly, they may have to face big consequences for what they do. Just because we understand that kids make mistakes doesn't alleviate the importance of trying to correct those mistakes. But we should always help our children understand that, even if they get punished for something, it isn't going to separate them from our love.

And somehow in the middle of all that, we must find a way to convey that *we're not perfect* either.

Again, I believe parents in the Christian community have an especially hard time owning up to this. I know of many parents who do a great job of modeling this idea of "nobody's perfect." But when I go through some of the letters and emails we get at Focus on the Family, I certainly get the impression that we expect an enormous amount from ourselves and our children. And when we fail as parents, we don't feel comfortable confessing our failures to our kids. What a shame, because embracing a model of imperfection is one of the best things we can do.

We've discussed how Christians understand, perhaps as well as anyone, our own sinful natures. We get that nobody's perfect. Sometimes we're able to translate that to our kids, to show them a model of grace and forgiveness even as we do our best to correct their mistakes.

But we find it hard, and understandably so, to admit our own weaknesses to our children. We want to be *great* role models for our kids. We want, in some ways, to be *perfect*, to show them how it's done.

But when we can't admit our own wrongdoing to our sons and daughters, particularly as fathers, it's like we put an unspoken asterisk on our "nobody's perfect" message — and an asterisk beside Christ's own saving grace on the cross. We tell our kids that nobody's perfect, but we're really whispering that nobody's perfect *except me*. Everybody makes mistakes *except me*. And when they get old enough to realize that you *do* make mistakes (and every child reaches that point), it makes them all the more aware of a sense of hypocrisy. It can damage your relationship with your child in a way that owning up to your shortfalls and saying "I'm sorry" could never do.

I get that it's hard to admit any sort of imperfection to your children, especially early in their lives when they think you can do no wrong. Part of us would love for them to go on thinking that for as long as possible. It's hard to admit our failures to other adults, so how can we come clean with our kids?

All in Good Time

Several years ago, the Calvary Chapel evangelist Raul Ries was speaking to about fifteen hundred men at a retreat. Right after coming on stage, he said, "Hey, before I get started, men, I want you to come on down here if you're addicted to pornography. I want you to come down right now, confess your sins, and let's get started right." Half the group came down — something like seven hundred guys. It was incredible.

But let's face it. That kind of transparency is rare, even in the church, where we're supposed to be supporting each other through everything. We do everything in secret now. We build a facade of perfection around us, while underneath the facade some very ugly things happen. We keep it all bottled up rather than confessing and expressing our issues to each other. Instead of saying, "Here are my failures. Here's where I'm weak. Can you help me be in control?" we cover them up.

No wonder so many people outside the faith see Christians in a poor light. We try so hard to project this perfection, which the world can't connect to. They look at Christians and see us as either freaks or liars. They say, "I don't believe them. They're hypocrites." And you know what? They're right. We don't live that life of perfection we pretend to live. We can't. You know why?

Because nobody's perfect, that's why.

Now, that doesn't mean we should spill out our guts to our kids when they're five. They don't necessarily need to hear about the time you tried pot in high school or about your sexual experiences in college. There may be a time and a place to talk with your kids about your less than God-honoring experiences, but sometimes what's in the past is better served staying there for a while.

But when it comes down to the mistakes you make today, particularly the moments you wrong your own children, it's important to confess and tell them you're sorry, just as you'd expect them to confess and apologize to you.

It's a wonderful model and an enriching moment to deal openly and honestly with your kids, to be able to say, "I'm sorry, I think I've offended you," or to ask, "Have I hurt you in some way? Have I embarrassed you? Have I in the last week made you angry?"

I know families who do this around the dinner table during a family chat. It has to be a safe environment in which kids can answer questions honestly, without fear of punishment. They teach the kids that it's safe to answer candidly and to transparently share their own feelings.

Parents need some training too. They have to resist the temptation to rationalize or correct their children. I know we feel strongly tempted to brush off a child's hurt and concerns, because when we do this exercise in my own house, I feel as tempted as anyone. I want to rationalize or explain why I did this or that. It's hard to ask a really frightening question — "Have I done anything this week to offend you?" — and then just accept the answer, particularly when your kids are twelve or thirteen or fourteen. So many things can offend kids who are that age.

It can be both hard and humbling. But it can also open the doors to an enriching honesty that'll pay huge dividends later on.

In our house, if the boys do something bad, we've been known to punish them through spanking. The punishment never gets too vigorous, because I can never bring myself to spank the kids with too much muscle. But I found it interesting to note how the boys responded differently to those moments of corporal punishment.

Troy would take his spanking just fine. "Okay, Dad, I'll do better next time," he'd say. "Bye!" — and off he'd go. Trent would take it more personally. But for a long time, I never realized how much it hurt him, not physically, but emotionally.

One night, when Trent was five or six, we disciplined him for something. He got a quick swat across the rump with a spoon. After it ended, he went to his room, crying more from defiance or embarrassment than from the pain. I gave him a few minutes, and then I followed him to his room, just to talk with him and encourage him, but he wouldn't talk to me. He'd only nod or shake his head.

I began to ask him questions.

"Are you feeling hurt?" I asked. He nodded his head.

"Have I wounded your spirit?" Again he nodded.

"Do you know what you did wrong?" He shook his head violently.

And then I said something that, in a way, surprises me even today.

"Can you write your answers for me?"

Slowly, sadly, he nodded. So I fetched a pad of paper and a pen, and I asked him a simple question that would likely contain a very, very difficult answer to read.

"How do you feel when I discipline you?" I asked.

Trent put pen to paper and scrawled out in his six-year-old letters the hardest answer of all.

"It feels like you don't love me."

His answer floored me. This little boy, angry, hurting, and afraid, was suffering in a way that I had never intended, forced to deal with a pain that had nothing to do with a swat on the behind and everything to do with a bruised heart.

It feels like you don't love me.

I could've nursed my own hurt in that moment. I could've

gotten defensive or even angry. Instead, I asked another question.

"Do you know that Daddy's not perfect?" He nodded his head yes.

"Do you know that what I'm here to do as a father is to help you be better?" Again, yes.

"And that you're here to help me be better?" Another nod.

My last question was very simple. Very straightforward. Very necessary.

"Can you forgive me?"

With that, Trent bloomed. He nodded his head one last time, and a smile edged its way onto his face. We hugged, and he started talking again. "Okay, Dad," he said. "Let's have dinner."

"He's Up Again"

From that point forward, whenever I had to discipline Trent, I'd stay away from physical punishment and instead take away privileges. I'd put away a toy he really enjoyed—for a day or two. Or maybe we'd take away his TV or video game time. He responds much better to these sorts of corrective methods.

This moment of honesty, as painful as it felt for both of us at the time, allowed me to tweak my own parenting to better serve Trent. I think it strengthened our relationship. The fact that I could admit my own shortcoming to Trent made our family better.

I'm still not perfect, of course. My boys know that all too well. When my kids were younger, I'd bluster. I didn't know how to manage my frustration. I didn't know how to remain calm. I never let it manifest itself in anything physical, but I'd show my anger, and it scared them—exactly what I wanted at the time. But now that I look back on it, I wonder *why*. Why did I want to scare them? Why would I want them to feel afraid of their own father?

I've improved a lot in that area. Now I find that I have to watch my sarcasm. My sense of humor can feel very cutting, and it can come at the expense of the people around me. It's probably my greatest weakness, and even though I'm getting better at catching myself, I don't always catch myself enough.

Those weaknesses of mine may reflect your own. Or maybe they don't. Maybe you have other problems or sins. Maybe you struggle with drinking or drugs. Maybe you have a dangerous sexual appetite. Maybe you work too hard, or not hard enough, or engage in slander or gossip. I suppose there are as many problems as there are fathers, and I can't name your problems. But I know you have one or two. We all do. We're all David. We're all Jim Daly. We're all imperfect.

This doesn't surprise God. He knows us and our problems. It's not really a question of *if* they'll trip us up, but *when* and *where* and *how badly*. We'll all fall, that's for certain. The question before us is this: Are we going to get back up?

Tony Evans begins his book *Kingdom Man* with this sentence: "A kingdom man is the kind of man that when his feet hit the floor each morning the devil says, 'Oh crap, he's up!' "[18]

I love that line. It inspires me. It helps me to understand that, even if I failed yesterday or the day before, I have another chance to get it right today. And if I fail today, another chance will come along tomorrow. Each day we get up determined to do our best as husbands and fathers and men, that's another defeat for the devil. Each day we get up ready to learn and grow from whatever comes our way, even our mistakes, that's a day we please our heavenly Father.

Are we living in such a way that, every morning, when we

get our feet out of bed and onto the ground the devil says, "Oh crap, he's up"? We're men. That's the sort of life we ought to live.

As Christ himself showed us, the fall doesn't matter as much as the ability to rise again.

────────── **TO THINK ABOUT** ──────────

1. What's the biggest mistake you made as a kid? How did your father or mother handle it? Do you think they had the right response? How would you have handled it differently as a parent?

2. If you're a father now, what's the biggest mistake you've made as a dad? Did you own up to it with your children?

3. How do you show your kids that you're not perfect? How do you prove to them that it's okay that they're not perfect?

Five

Love and Duty

THE NIGHT OF MY MOTHER'S FUNERAL — THE NIGHT HANK left us — felt like the longest night of my life. My mom, the only real stability I had ever known, was gone. My stepfather had packed up the house and taken almost everything, leaving my siblings and me practically destitute. Even my oldest brother, Mike, left me that day to return to his ship. He was in the Navy. And the roof over our heads wouldn't remain ours for long either. That night, the four of us slept on the floor of our empty old house, lying on and under whatever clothes we could find.

The following morning, my siblings began to pick up the pieces and try to build a new tomorrow for all of us.

The night before, my brother Dave had found a place for three of us (himself, Dee Dee, and me) to live. (Mike had just reported for duty, and Kim was out on her own as well.) Dave's friends, the Reils, had agreed to let us stay with them. So on the morning after my mother's funeral, three of us piled into Dave's car and headed east into the California desert and toward the parched, dusty town of Morongo Valley.

The thermometer already hovered in the mid-eighties by

the time we started down the highway. The car had no air-conditioning, so we had rolled down all of our windows, but the warm air that buffeted us didn't do much to cool us off. Bugs spattered across the windshield glass in wet thumps. "Those bugs should've known better than to play tag with the windshield," my mother might've said had she been there. But she wasn't, and she'd never be here again.

The road curled on and on, through a land without water, through a valley of rocks, dust, and flies. I didn't feel much of anything right then. I suppose I was suffering something like shell shock. I sat in the backseat, blank, without a clear idea of where I was going. I had little hope that things would improve with the Reils, or that Mr. Reil would provide an upgrade over my deeply flawed father or my strict and distant stepdad. I felt terribly discouraged. This would be just another stop for me, one of many unrewarding, unfulfilling stops.

But I had no clue just how bad, or weird, things would soon get.

I've changed the first names of the Reil family to save those who are still with us a little embarrassment, but the stories are all too real, and they begin on their funky five-acre plot of land on the outskirts of Morongo Valley. Bob Reil had worked as a butcher at Hormel Foods for years, toiling on the assembly line cutting up pork until a dead pig slipped from a hook and fell on Mr. Reil's head and shoulders. I don't know how he wound up in Morongo Valley, but I'd guess he probably took a small disability settlement, bought this little homestead, and survived as well as he, his wife, and their four boys could. They grew most of their own food and had a nice vegetable garden that provided whatever greenery they needed. It seemed they also had countless rabbits and chickens to slaughter for the evening meal's main course.

From the minute I saw Mr. Reil, I could see he was ... odd — short and wiry and without a single tooth in his mouth. A nervous little man. He had dentures but didn't always wear them, so his chin often stuck out in a point and his lips curled up over his toothless gums. I hardly ever saw him without a cigarette, never mind his three heart attacks. He looked, in a way, like a stereotypical hillbilly. Part of me saw it as just par for the course. I went from an embarrassing drunk father to an embarrassing detached stepfather to an embarrassing hick foster father. And it became clear early on that Mr. Reil (I never called him anything but Mr. Reil) had no more love for me than Hank did.

I appreciated that the Reils took us in, but I'm pretty sure they did it for the money. The state provided funds to foster parents, and I guess they used that cash to supplement Mr. Reil's disability income. I imagine they needed the money, and maybe they held a certain amount of resentment toward us Dalys because of that. We constantly reminded them of their need, and what they had to do to fill that need.

Not that they had a lot of spare room to fill. Dave and I eventually slept in the same room with the four Reil boys — nineteen-year-old Dale, eighteen-year-old Kevin, fifteen-year-old Steve, and Ben, who at eight was just a year younger than I was. At first, I thought the Reil children might prove to be a bright spot. My brother, Dave, and Kevin had become close friends, which explains how we wound up with them in the first place. Kevin, handsome and outgoing, didn't hang around much, since both he and my brother worked while in high school. As for me, I thought maybe I could play with Steve and Ben. But the whole situation collapsed into a nightmare. It turned out that Steve was discovering his same-sex attraction, and he showed an uncomfortable interest in me, despite my tender nine years of age. Ben concerned me too. His klepto-mania drove him to go underneath my cot whenever I left the room and swipe the few remaining toys and possessions I still owned. I found it nearly impossible to get him to return them. Whenever I'd plead for Mrs. Reil's help, she naturally believed her son. Ben, after all, would never take anything that wasn't his! I, on the other hand, was just an unwanted houseguest completely unworthy of trust.

Ironically, someone later told me that Ben eventually got in trouble for fraud. It made me think about the old days and smile a little. Could I have been his first victim?

I could've used a father back then, any semblance of a father. Even Hank might've been a step up. At least Hank paid some attention to me. He cared on some level about what I did, even if his interest came with a sharply critical edge. But Mr. Reil barely acknowledged my existence, especially in the first two weeks. He rarely spoke to me. It seemed he didn't know, or care, that I was even there.

But when he finally did pay attention to me, I wished he hadn't.

"Jimmy, Come Over Here"

I already mentioned that the Reils' rabbits and chickens weren't there just for the ambience or as family pets. On most nights, they became our dinner. If Mr. Reil, the former butcher, knew how to do anything, he knew how to kill and cut up animals.

About two weeks after I arrived at the Reils', one afternoon, as I wandered around the grounds trying to figure out the boundaries of the property, I strayed near the chicken coop. I saw Mr. Reil and Ben, a stump between them, and Mr. Reil holding an ax. Ben clutched a good-sized chicken, its head on the stump. And as I watched, Mr. Reil raised the ax and brought it down.

Thwump!

I watched, horrified (and probably a little curious), as the chicken's head fell to the ground, its eyes still blinking and its mouth moving noiselessly. The body of the chicken thrashed around, doing somersaults in the dirt. The chicken's heart still beat furiously, blood pumping out of the bird's neck like a fountain, spraying its white feathers with blood. I'd never witnessed such a wild and surreal scene. And at just nine years old I remember laughing a little, just to cover up my nervousness.

That laugh attracted the attention of Mr. Reil. He looked at me and motioned for me to come on over.

"Jimmy, come over here," he said, giving me a toothless grin. "You gotta cut the head off a chicken."

For kids raised on a farm, this might not have seemed like a big deal. But for me, who'd grown up in metropolitan Los Angeles, I couldn't believe the demand. Just two weeks before, I had buried my mother. I felt alone and afraid in a strange, strange place. And now a man — my foster parent, the guy charged by the state to give me a little stability — had asked me to cut off a chicken's head.

I shook my head. "I don't think I want to do that," I told him, backing away.

"No, you gotta come over here and do it," Mr. Reil insisted. "It'll make a man outta you."

It went on like that for a little bit, Mr. Reil pressuring, me refusing, Ben grinning all the while. Finally, Mr. Reil put the ax in my hand and got the chicken ready. I didn't want to do it. I felt scared to the point of getting sick. I'd never killed anything bigger than a bug. But Mr. Reil wouldn't let me leave. I resisted and resisted, but then it got to the point where I felt that, if I resisted anymore, I might make Mr. Reil angry. And if he got angry enough, what might he do? I wasn't his flesh and blood. Would he hurt me? Throw me out of the house? And if he did, where would I go? How long can you say no to someone like that before you risk breaking the relationship forever? How long do I keep saying no before I don't have this person's trust anymore? Nine-year-olds don't have the resources to answer such heavy questions.

So I raised the ax and did it. I walked out of the chicken coop with blood on my hands, quite literally. Afterward, I didn't feel scared or sad or angry. I felt *guilty*. I'd taken a life, an animal life, sure, but a life all the same. And even though the chicken would've found its way to the Reils' kitchen sooner or later, it still sickened me to think that I sealed its fate by the swing of my child-sized arm.

Hard Lessons

I believe Mr. Reil meant well. In his world he looked at me and saw a nine-year-old city boy, a little too proper, maybe a little spoiled. He wanted me to grow up a little. Just like he said, Mr. Reil wanted me to become a man, or more of a man, by cutting off the head of a chicken.

But even though Mr. Reil might have correctly identified some things about me (I *was* a city kid and, yes, a little spoiled), the incident proved far too much for me. A nine-year-old is *not* a man. If there were ever a chance that I could've felt at home at the Reils', that chance ended that afternoon.

Just as I worried about damaging my relationship with Mr. Reil, Mr. Reil took action to splinter his relationship with me.

Many fathers fall into the same trap, even if they don't use a live chicken as a catalyst.

One of the traditional duties of a father — one that, surprisingly, hasn't changed too much — is that of primary disciplinarian. While moms tend to dole out discipline more often, dads often get perceived as the ultimate seat of authority within a household. The old cliché — "just wait till your father gets home" — remains true in many families.

"Fathers tend to be more willing than mothers to confront their children and enforce discipline," write Kyle and Marsha Kline Pruett in their book *Partnership Parenting*, "leaving their children with the impression that they in fact *have* more authority."[19] While moms tend to try reasoning with their children and show more flexibility in discipline, dads tend to set down rules and expect their kids to obey them — or else.

But while this fatherly authority forms a natural part of many families' inner workings — and, I think, forms part of God's plan for the family — fathers must wield that authority carefully and consistently. All of the discipline and authority you hold, and all of the lessons you'd like to teach through that authority, will do a child little good if they don't also feel your love and affection.

Don't take my word for it, or that of child psychologists. The Bible itself tells a story about a father's love for his sons, and what can happen if one of the sons doesn't see that love.

The "Other" Son

Most of us know the story of the prodigal son, the parable Jesus told as recounted in Luke 15. "There was a man who had two sons," the story begins.

The younger son, an irresponsible wild-child, asked his dad for his inheritance early and then squandered it all on "wild living." After all of his money dried up, the younger son had no choice but to crawl back to his father's house and beg to work for him as a hired hand. But when the son returned, the father did more than take his son in and put him to work; as soon as he saw the boy, the father ran out to meet him, throwing his arms around him in a huge bear hug. He decided to throw a massive feast in honor of his returning child. "For this son of mine was dead and is alive again; he was lost and is found."

It's a beautiful story. Through this relationship between father and son, Jesus shows us what it really means to be a father in the mold of our heavenly Father — One who loves, no matter what, and One with boundless compassion and capacity for forgiveness.

But sometimes we lose sight of that other son in the background, the one who Jesus says got so peeved at the father's favoritism that he refused to join the feast.

"Look, these many years I have served you, and I never disobeyed your command, yet you never gave me a young goat, that I might celebrate with my friends," the older brother says, seeming to nearly spit out the accusations and hurt. "But when this son of yours came, who has devoured your property with prostitutes, you killed the fattened calf for him!" (Luke 15:29 – 30 ESV).

The main message Jesus intends to convey through the older brother is, of course, a spiritual one: We should not envy God's boundless grace, because he loves us no matter what. But when I hear this story, another underlying question comes to mind.

What kind of fathers would these two sons become?

I believe that both of them, if they existed in real life, would have grown up to mirror their own father, just as all of us tend to do. But they would have become two very different fathers, because each saw his father in a very different way. One, the younger son, saw a great deal of love and forgiveness in his father. And I imagine that when he had children, he would show his own kids that same unconditional love, showering them with forgiveness when they needed forgiveness. But I believe the older son would have become legalistic and distant, since that was the father *he* knew. The older son served his father well, and so he might expect his children to serve him well too. If the father never gave much to the older son, perhaps that son would have a hard time giving to his own children.

We learn so much from our parents. Even lessons we'd rather not learn.

Discipline Is Good, but ...

Developmental psychologists describe four distinct types of parenting styles, first cataloged by psychologist Diana Baumrind in the 1960s.[20] There are *uninvolved parents*, undemanding mothers and fathers who seem to spend as little time and effort on their children as possible. There are *permissive parents*, who may give their children love and affection but have very few expectations of them. *Authoritative parents*, the best sort of parents, according to Baumrind, have rules and guidelines in place, but every rule has a reason for existence and every guideline comes seasoned with love. Baumrind writes, "Their disciplinary methods are supportive, rather than punitive. They want their children to be assertive as well as socially responsible, and self-regulated as well as cooperative."

The fourth parenting style outlined by Baumrind is *authoritarian parenting*, which features abundant rules and punishment. Authoritarian parents have rigid and unforgiving attitudes, and while they dole out discipline both swiftly and surely, the rules that trigger punishment often confuse the children (sometimes the parents themselves barely grasp their own rules). You might call this the "because I said so" mode of parenting — often the only rationale such parents give their kids for why they should obey a given rule.

As a general observation, each of these parenting styles tends to yield certain kinds of results. Kids raised by permissive parents, for instance, tend to be pretty mellow but have low self-control. Children in authoritarian households often behave well, but they lack the resourcefulness of some of their peers and tend to have more trouble socializing.

Sometimes kids in those authoritarian situations grow increasingly meek and compliant as time goes on. But sometimes they grow angry and frustrated until something just snaps.

Mr. Reil fit into the "uninvolved father" type in my life. He rarely paid attention to me. But that moment in the chicken coop, he became very authoritarian. The showdown over the chicken became a classic "because I said so" moment between us, and something did snap for me — my hope that Mr. Reil could ever become anything close to the father figure I needed.

Hank might've been the poster dad for authoritarian parenting, the guy those psychologists had in mind. He had rules for *everything*, and heaven help you if you broke one of them. If I used a blanket and then left it without folding it up, he'd make me fold it over and over again. At least he was consistent. He always followed through and never backed down. And as the honest and naive kid I was, I'd always just accept his discipline and do my punishment to get it over with.

My sister, Kim, didn't comply so readily.

One day, when my family lived in Long Beach, California, Kim, Dee Dee, and I were playing Frisbee out in our backyard.

But at eight years old, I didn't always have the best aim. One of my throws went really off course, right through a glass window in the small garage door.

As the sound of breaking glass reverberated off the concrete floor, Hank stormed out of the house and started hollering at us, using some very colorful language. "Who broke that [blankety-blank] window?" he shouted.

I felt scared to death to confess, but as a good kid, I didn't want to lie. (Plus, there were witnesses.) Just as I mustered the courage to confess, Kim shouted, "I did it! What you gonna do about it?"

"I'll tell you what I'm going to do," Hank blustered. "I'm going to tear into you!" And Hank literally started chasing Kim around the backyard, both of them cursing and flipping each other off. It looked like a profane Three Stooges movie or something.

And then after they ran around the backyard for a couple of minutes, Kim opened the gate to the front, ran through it, and took off down the street, Hank in hot pursuit.

I didn't see her for a year. She literally just ran away from home.

Rule One: Cut Down on the Rules

Psychologists say that authoritative parents, not authoritarian ones, seem to raise the healthiest children. Kids need firm guidelines. They thrive under reasonable expectations. And sometimes when sons or daughters break a rule, they need to be punished. But I think parents, especially fathers, cross over from *authoritative* into *authoritarian* quickly when a rule gets broken. They channel their inner Hank when that broken rule becomes a bigger priority than the child who broke it. When we grow too dogmatic over our punishments, when we refuse to listen to our children's explanations, or when we fail to understand the context behind the behavior, we get into trouble.

Sometimes we forget that our rules, guidelines, and expectations are merely tools to help build something much more important — strong, resourceful, and considerate men and women. So if we have rules that won't help our children learn and grow, we have to ask ourselves, *Is that particular rule even necessary?*

I know such a question is far easier to say or write than to practice. The line between *authoritative* and *authoritarian* doesn't always seem clear or distinct. In the Daly household, we sometimes have a hard time figuring it out.

Brady Boyd, senior pastor of New Life Church in Colorado Springs, came into the studio the other day to discuss his book, *Sons and Daughters: Spiritual Orphans Finding Our Way Home.* We spent some time talking about his own son and daughter and how he tries to emphasize what he calls a covenant relationship in the home. I particularly wanted to hear how he tries to keep his household rules to a minimum. Sure, they embrace a handful of core rules, but he says he doesn't want to overload children with expectations and guidelines. The more rules they have to follow, the more opportunities they have to break one. And every broken rule can open the door for the child to feel like a failure, to hear how he or she doesn't measure up. Kids shouldn't have to confront their failure so much every day.

Brady told how some families even have chalkboards or whiteboards filled with the home's rules and regulations. I started laughing — because we're one of those families! We actually have behavioral guidelines hanging up in our house, with Scripture references and everything. "We will treat everybody with honesty — Proverbs 12:22," one reads. I couldn't help but cringe when Brady nailed us like that.

Of course, Brady would probably agree with the *spirit* behind the rules we have in our household. I'm sure he's raising his children to be honest too. It's a good rule. There are many good rules. But too much of a good thing can hurt kids just as much as too much chocolate ice cream or too many video games or too much homework can. We need balance. We need moderation. It can be as problematic to have too many rules as to have no rules at all.

So here's the challenge facing us fathers: How can we create a home based on love and respect, not on rules? How can we help our children understand the purpose behind the *principles* we ask them to follow but not get sidetracked by the rules on the wall? How can we best teach our kids that we love them, even if they break a rule?

Troubleshooting

While Jean and I haven't taken the rules off our wall, we do try to be authoritative without being authoritarian. And we do it by using a number of commonsense tools.

For instance, when the kids do something wrong, we try not to overcomplicate or overdramatize the behavior. We try to remember that most kids their age make the same kinds of mistakes or engage in similar misbehavior. We all know that children go through phases. Lying or talking back may just be part of a phase. That doesn't make it right, of course. That doesn't mean you avoid taking steps to correct the problem. But it does help keep us fathers from overreacting.

We also categorize the issues and place them mentally in

certain levels or tiers. Jean and I do this informally. Taking a cookie before dinner might fall into a tier one category, while lying becomes much more serious, maybe a tier three issue. Categorizing problems like this allows us to relax a little on the less serious problems. If *everything* looks severe to you, then you have a bigger problem on your hands. Your parenting style may be crossing over into the authoritarian realm — a very unhealthy place.

Now, these tiers can cause their own problems. Maybe you and your wife don't agree with the seriousness, or with the tier, of a given problem. Maybe you can't decide whether something qualifies as a tier one or a tier three issue. Jean and I have the same disagreements. It's a natural offshoot of being a parent, I think. We're all different, and so we have different takes on what qualifies as serious. The important thing is to work through these issues as a couple. Talk about it and find a solution you both can live with.

With my background, I might have a different sense over what to consider really "serious" in a family. When you run away from home over a broken window, that's serious. When you steal toys from your foster brother and lie about it, that's serious. When you're a teenager making passes at a nine-year-old boy, that's serious.

But don't sweat the small stuff.

When I begin to get upset over a minor problem, my boys often call me on it. Troy's especially good at this. If he sloshes milk out of his cereal bowl on the kitchen floor and sees my temperature rise, he'll say, "Dad, it's only a little milk." And when he says it so plainly, I realize he's right. It *is* only a little milk. And once I reach that point, I realize that Troy's parroting what I've already taught him: *Don't sweat the small stuff.*

They've learned an important lesson that I sometimes have trouble retaining.

Tether of Love

I had some authoritarian father figures growing up. Hank had his rigid rules and tedious punishments — hanging up that unhung coat one hundred times. Mr. Reil had his chicken and his refusal to let a little nine-year-old orphan off the hook. Perhaps they both meant well. But when I think about my time with them, I don't have many good memories. I don't remember the lessons they tried to teach me. I remember the pain. The confusion. The anger. Hanging up that coat didn't make me any neater. Beheading that chicken didn't make me any manlier. Those experiences taught me only to never repeat them with my own boys.

Over time, I've come to picture parents' relationships with their children as something like a playground tetherball. You, as the parent, are the pole. You're not going anywhere. Your child is the ball. And the rope connecting you — the tether — is the love you share for each other. Your mutual affection is what connects you.

In tetherball, the ball whirls around the pole, sometimes drawing closer, sometimes spinning farther away, which mimics your relationship with your sons and daughters. At times you'll draw close to your children. Sometimes they'll feel more distant. As long as you've got that tether of love connecting both of you, however, they'll never entirely leave you.

But when the tether breaks, the ball just flies away. It's lost.

Neither rules nor judgment does anything to keep the ball tethered to the pole. The only thing that keeps the ball tethered to the pole is love.

It becomes so obvious when you think about it in terms of our own lives. When we think about our mothers and fathers, we may appreciate many of the things they taught us. But if we had a loving relationship with our parents and we remember the reasons we loved them and their love for us, we don't often think about rules or lessons or discipline. We think of the times we smiled and laughed together. We think of the games we played. The walks we took. The hugs. The bedtime stories.

That's what love looks like. That's what keeps the ball tethered to the tether.

I know some people will say, "Wait a minute; you're just passive." But I reject that notion. I teach my boys lots of lessons, and sometimes I need to discipline them. But you don't want to oversteer or overcorrect. You don't want to become so egregious in your discipline that your kids find it hard to love you anymore.

And don't think it can't happen. Focus on the Family's mailbags overflow with stories of those whose tether with their own parents or with their own children broke. It doesn't happen all at once, but it does happen. And when it does, it's a catastrophe. When the love gets crushed out of them, you have a big job ahead of you, much bigger than correcting a behavioral problem.

One of my favorite fathers is a man named Danie van den Heever, a South African businessman. When you look at how to balance love and discipline with your children, few people model it better.

Go to Danie's house for dinner, and you'll see a father with arms always open in love and friendship, even if he's in the middle of giving a stern rebuke. One night during a visit, I watched as Danie's son, Rudy, picked on his sister, making her very upset.

"Rudy, Rudy, Rudy," Danie said in his Afrikaans accent, smiling all the while. "Come, come. Sit here. Let's talk about this. Why are you doing this to your sister? Tell me, what's going on?"

He did it beautifully. No condemnation, no rebuke. There came no swift-as-lightning punishment for breaking a rule or doing something wrong. Danie validated Rudy as a person and as his much-loved son. He opened the way to dialogue so he as a father could get a better understanding of the situation. And he also let Rudy know — without an angry word, scowl, or slap of Rudy's hand — that he couldn't accept Rudy's behavior.

What an amazing way — a fatherly way, even a godly way — of drawing a daughter or son into a discussion without slapping them down. And because Danie had such a loving and open-handed attitude, the child responded with the same sort of kindness: "Tell me, Daddy, how am I not pleasing you?"

It was a thing of beauty.

How do we express our love for our kids so they know it's real, authentic, and unconditional? How can we maintain that tether of love?

Sometimes we parents get called on to maintain that tether through some horrible, even unimaginable circumstances. Children sometimes do far worse things than pick on a little sister, steal a cookie at suppertime, or get an F on a report card. Sometimes children, despite their best efforts, get into some real tier three problems. Drugs. Alcohol. Promiscuity. Difficulties with the law.

In those circumstances, they sometimes move beyond your rules and discipline. You ground them, and they sneak away. You punish them, and they laugh it off. They might run down the street and away from everything you believe in, just as Kim ran away from Hank. And the only thing you have left is that tether — the moments you've shared, the love you've shown. The tether is the last thing that holds you together.

If your children find themselves in a dark, dark place, that tether can pull them out. That tether gives you the ability to put your arm around them and say, "I care about you. And I'm always, *always* going to be here for you."

That's love. That's the foundation to everything you do as a parent. And Scripture calls it the right foundation.

Sometimes, of course, no matter what you do, the tether gets severed from the other end. Sometimes the prodigals don't come back. But very often, if you remain attentive to your relationship and that tether of love, they do return. And when you see them on the horizon as they walk back home, your heart will flood with joy and gratitude. What was dead is alive again. What was lost is found.

TO THINK ABOUT

1. As a child, did you ever feel pressured to do something before you felt ready? Did you wind up doing it? Were you glad you did it, or did it hurt you in some way?

2. What rules do you have in your family? Which of those rules do you consider the most important? Do any seem less important?

3. How did you get punished as a child? Did you consider it fair? If you have children, how do you punish them? Do you see it as effective?

Six

Mr. Reliable

Most men, I believe, keep score. We like to know who's winning and who's losing, whether on the softball diamond, at the golf course, or in the boardroom. We measure ourselves against others, against the clock, or even against an internal (and often highly subjective) yardstick. It can seem a little crazy at times.

It's not enough to know we're doing a good job at work — are we doing a better job than the person in the cubicle next to us? It's not enough to have a nice lawn — does it look nicer than the Foleys' down the street? We get so wrapped up in performance that everything becomes a competition, a referendum not just on how we're doing but on *who we are.*

Except when it comes to our kids.

All too often, we let that area of our life slide. We may find a low performance in that area acceptable because (we think) nobody's really looking.

But that's not true, is it? Our kids are watching. Our kids *always* watch. And while they might not measure winners or losers, comparing this dad with that one, they do keep score

—even if neither you nor they realize it. And when the final buzzer sounds and their childhood ends, sometimes we find we've *all* lost.

Of all the things that can hurt us in the eyes of our children, our own inconsistencies could be the most glaring and hurtful. If the ideal dad resembles my picture of a strong, unshakable oak tree, many of us can sometimes look more like reeds in the water. We bend. We break. We float downstream. We tend to dry up and wither away if the conditions don't stay just right. We might not be there next year. Next month. Sometimes even sticking around next week becomes an iffy proposition. Our kids can't count on us. We can't be trusted.

Our children won't really know which sort of father we are —an oak or a reed—until we reveal ourselves. And when that moment happens, they'll never forget it.

In Deep Water

I've already talked a lot in this book about my birth father, and my stories haven't sounded the happiest. But my dad was not a bad man. In fact, my first memories of him remain full of joy.

He worked a lot of jobs in his life, but the first I remember was that of the Helms Bakery deliveryman. Back then in Southern California, bakery trucks rivaled ice cream trucks in number. Bread, doughnuts, and those cool candy necklaces filled the backs of those trucks—shelves and bins full of all kinds of treats. Being a deliveryman probably didn't pay very well. But when you're four years old, like I was, the doughnut deliveryman seems only a half step below superhero. I felt like, "Wow, that's the coolest job a dad could have."

And when the day's work was done, Dad would come home, sometimes with a doughnut in his hand, which he'd hand over to me. He'd sit down and I'd hop on his lap, and he'd run his fingers through my hair. I'll always remember and cherish the sensation of those wide fingers running over my scalp.

Some of my brothers and sisters don't remember it as fondly as I do, if at all. Maybe that's because I was so much younger than the rest of them (Dee Dee, the next youngest, is six years older than me), but he had an affection for me that he didn't seem to show to the rest of them. My older brothers sometimes got into fistfights with him. But he loved me, I knew without a doubt. And I loved him with the full, nearly bursting heart that only a four-year-old can have. No matter how my brothers and sisters saw him, I saw him differently. I saw him as my oak, the strength I could lean on.

One sticky summer day when I was around four or five, the Daly family trekked over to a local pool to cool off. My dad came too. He didn't swim much, but on those rare jaunts to the pool, he'd sit at a poolside table, cigarette in hand, and watch his kids swim. And since I didn't know how to swim, I'd venture down the stairs near the shallow end to go in up to my chest. With the deep end, I got more cautious. I'd dangle my feet in the water and kick a little, feeling the cool, chlorinated water splash onto my shins.

These days, most parents probably wouldn't let their kids hang around the deep end unless the children knew at least how to dog-paddle. Or, if they did, they probably would slap a life vest or some water wings on them, just in case. You never know what might happen. And honestly, I think most kids, if they don't know how to swim, would stay well away from the deep end. To little kids, dangerous things like that can almost seem like whirlpools, ready to suck in a poor unsuspecting child who gets too close.

But I didn't worry. After all, I knew my dad was watching

me. That big, strong, fearless man wouldn't let any harm come to me. I trusted him.

And so I watched as the sun glinted off the water and listened to my brothers and sisters splash and laugh. And then, suddenly, I felt two strong hands grab me around my middle, pressing into my ribs. Somebody lifted me up like I was a runaway elevator.

And I heard my father's voice behind me, strong and maybe a little slurred.

"It's time to learn how to swim," he said.

I felt the fingers uncurl from my middle, and I went flying. Falling. I hit the water with a smack and sank into the blue water, nine feet of it folding over me.

I don't remember the water going into my lungs. I don't remember panicking or feeling scared that I was going to die. I just remember crying. Crying underwater.

Thankfully, my brother Mike dove in, grabbed me, and pulled me to the edge of the pool. I held on to the edge, coughing and sputtering and still crying — crying *hard*. And I thought, over and over, *Why? Why would he do that?* I couldn't understand.

At that moment, my heart began to change toward my dad. I no longer saw him as the oak of my imagination. He didn't provide me with the reassuring strength I needed.

I didn't stop loving him. I didn't close up my heart entirely. But from then on, I kept my guard up with him. I understood that I couldn't rely on him. I couldn't trust him.

The Inconsistent Father

In a way, my father was ahead of his time.

As I grew up, fathers were seen as stabilizing influences

in most families — the old, solid oak tree I described earlier. True, they didn't get as involved with raising children as dads are expected to be today, but they remained stalwart figures at home, providing for and protecting their wives and children.

Many would-be fathers today refuse to take root. They often run from their responsibilities. Only 63 percent of children grew up in a two-parent household in 2010, according to a study from the Massachusetts Institute of Technology. That's down from 82 percent in 1970.[21] In most cases, it's the father who leaves, abandoning his children and making it far more likely they'll struggle with poverty, instability, and discipline trouble. According to a 2009 study by the National Center for Fathering, seven out of ten people call the physical absence of fathers "the most significant family or social problem facing America."[22]

Both President George W. Bush and President Barack Obama stressed the importance of family and fatherhood. President Obama, in his 2013 State of the Union address, said, "What makes you a man isn't the ability to conceive a child; it's having the courage to raise one." President Bush told me after I interviewed him that "the breakdown of the family is the number one threat our nation faces." I think most people know, in their heart of hearts, that unhealthy families make for unhealthy societies. Politics aside, *these* men know it.

But even when fathers stick around, they may still cause trouble.

Most of us probably know people who had unreliable or unapproachable fathers. You may have grown up with such a father yourself. These dads spend most of their time and energy at work and rarely interact with their kids. They communicate with their children only through yelling or arguing. They often see their kids only while drunk or stoned.

And then you have volatile dads, like mine, who act erratically. One minute they're fun and loving, the next they're red in the face and furious. They might swing from apologetic to apoplectic in the space of an hour. They might buy you an ice cream cone and then take it away from you and eat it. They might throw you up in the air and leave you squealing in joy, or toss you in the deep end and leave you crying in terror.

While statistics tell us that two-parent households have loads of advantages over one-parent homes, we know, anecdotally, that fathers must be more than physically present; they need to be *fully* there — mentally, emotionally, and spiritually. I once heard someone say, "Nothing — no one, no organization, no well-intended school system, no government — can fully replace a missing parent, an uninvolved parent, an overwhelmed parent, or a parent who simply doesn't care. There is no replacement for a parent." And I completely agree with this statement.

My father was all of those at various times. He was uninvolved and overwhelmed. Sometimes it seemed as though he didn't care. And sometimes he went missing, replaced by a monster I couldn't understand at all.

Hammered

I was five when the monster came home with a ball-peen hammer.

I don't think Dad and Mom were still together by then. Not really. They had hit a rough patch, problems caused by my father's drinking maybe. No doubt they had other troubles that a five-year-old had no way of understanding. He probably paid his share of the rent, collected his mail, and maybe slept there.

But I don't remember seeing him around much. He'd ceased to be a big part of our lives.

My mom had left for the evening, but all of us kids sat in the small living room with the pea-green walls, watching television or something. And then the door flew open with a boom.

"Where is she?" my dad bellowed, the words blurred and sticky with alcohol. "*Where is she?*"

His cheeks, chin, and neck looked covered in scruff, his eyes puffy and red. He carried a ball-peen hammer, the varnished oak handle disappearing into my dad's huge, white-knuckled fist.

This wasn't my father — at least, not the father who ran his fingers through my hair. Not even the father who threw me into a pool. This was a beast, a monster gone mad. He thrashed through the house like a bear with rabies, growling and howling in rage and pain.

"This is what I'm gonna do to your mother!"

BAM! The hammer smashed into the drywall, leaving a ragged black hole.

"I'm gonna kill her!"

BAM! Another blow. Paintings shuddered. Furniture shook. Another inky-black gash tore through the dull green wall.

What happened over the next few seconds blurs in my memory. I don't remember exactly who hustled me into Mom and Dad's bedroom, the only bedroom accessible without fleeing past my unhinged father. All I know is that's where I ended up, under the covers in my parents' bed, the blankets pulled up to my chin. When you're little and scared, you look for any sort of protection you can find, and for me that night, that blanket, held tightly against my neck like a fluffy shield, felt like my only possible source of salvation.

I learned later what happened on the other side of my parents' bedroom door. Dave somehow escaped the house, crawling out of a window and running all the way to the bowling alley where my mom worked. My sisters watched my father as his rage rose and ebbed like the surf. Eventually, he settled into his brown corduroy recliner, one hand hooked to a jug of Gallo wine, the other still wrapped around the hammer. And as he muttered and swore in the chair, swigging the Gallo and sloshing it on his shirt, he struck the floor with the hammer.

But I saw none of that. I'd been left alone, feeling disconnected and vulnerable. All I heard, all I knew, were mysterious, mostly unintelligible noises — the rise and fall of my dad's slurred, sour voice, mumbling words like *mother* and *kill*. The high-pitched, sobbing pleas of my sisters. The sharp, thunderclap bang of the hammer on the carpet.

Thump.

Thump.

Thump.

Violence at Home

I honestly doubt that my dad would've ever hurt me. I just don't think he was that kind of guy. As I've explained, maybe it was because I was the youngest (by far) of all his children. He doted on me in a strange way. He showed more affection to me and my sister, Kim, than to anyone else in the family.

But even sober he looked intimidating, standing six foot five and always in good shape. And when my dad got drunk or angry (or, worse, both), he'd threaten to hurt *somebody*. I never saw much of this myself, but my brothers and sisters remember: One night, in a drunken rage, my father threatened to hurt my mom. My oldest brother, Mike, got between the two of them. "If you touch her, I'll kill you," he told my dad. He was fourteen at the time and stood more than six feet tall — even at that young age, a formidable presence.

Perhaps nothing characterizes an inconsistent father more than physical abuse. Most, after all, don't get violent all the time. Some can feel awful after they've lashed out, apologizing repeatedly and promising never to do it again. Many abusive parents use a variety of psychological techniques to keep their victims off guard or to minimize their own actions. And at the very least, the victim always has to deal with internal inconsistency. How do you reconcile the idea of a man who tells you he loves you with the one who threatens to pound you if you spill your cereal? Such disconcerting messages leave kids confused and afraid, even if the violence never gets aimed at them.

Children raised in violent homes don't typically fare well, and it's not only the physical harm that puts kids at risk. The mental and emotional damage can take an even greater toll. According to a Child Welfare Information Gateway resource published in 2009, children who see or experience violence in the home are more likely to be aggressive, depressed, or antisocial.[23] They are more likely to struggle in school too, having difficulty on tests designed to measure verbal, motor, and cognitive skills and showing less ability to solve problems or resolve conflicts. Boys who grow up in abusive homes are twice as likely to adopt those same abusive and violent behaviors when they become parents, according to the National Coalition Against Domestic Violence (NCADV), thus extending a tragic cycle of abuse for generations.[24] For children raised in such homes, violence can feel normal. *This is how adults solve problems,* they rationalize. And so that's how they try to solve their own troubles.

I would like to say that violence and abuse don't affect good families, particularly good Christian families. But Christians have no immunity against these problems. In fact, statistically, I doubt we'd find much difference. One out of every four women in the United States becomes a victim of domestic violence at some point in their lives. A staggering 1.3 million women are attacked by their husband or partner every year. According to the NCADV, anywhere from 30 to 60 percent of those abusive husbands wind up being abusive fathers too.[25]

With numbers like that, I have a hard time believing that it stops outside the church door.

Focus on the Family occasionally hears stories about inconsistent, violent, and even abusive fathers who have been helped by our organization. Not long ago, we received a testimony from a California school principal, who told us of a father who attended a series of classes in our "Raising Highly Capable Kids" initiative. Here is this father's summary of his experience:

> *I want to let you know that before coming to these classes here at the school, I was an alcoholic. I was abusive to my wife and abusive to my children. I didn't know how to talk to them. My family was in turmoil. But since I've taken these classes, I've changed the way I talk to my wife. I no longer yell and physically abuse her, but instead we now take time to talk to each other. Now that we have better communication, it has led to better communication with my children. Before, I didn't know how to stop and talk and ask them, "How was your day? What did you learn in school?" Now I talk to them. There's no more fighting. There's no more turmoil at home. I am a better man because of these classes, and I like*

*myself now. You are my second family, and my wife wants me
to tell you thank you because I have changed the way I am.
My family is so happy. If it weren't for these classes, I don't
know where I'd be today.*

The man sounds painfully familiar to me. He reminds me
of my father, a man who didn't know how to be a good husband and dad — and maybe sometimes didn't even know why
he should try. Not until he got the help he needed.

But many, many fathers never get that help, that wake-up
call that can put their lives on a better trajectory. Sometimes
the story has an unhappy ending.

Taken Away

My childhood memories sometimes take on the character of
old photos — parts of the picture are crisp and unmistakable,
while the edges of the picture blur and fade.

The night my dad came home swinging a ball-peen hammer was one of those nights. Some of what happened that night
feels indistinct and hazy, almost like a dream. But my fear feels
as sharp and cold today as it did fifty years ago. As I lay in my
parents' bed — the bed they shared in happier times, the bed
they'd never share again — and held that blanket over my throat
and up to my chin, my eyes wide, my breathing staccato-quick,
I felt totally isolated. So vulnerable. I had no oak tree to lean
on for comfort, but only a drunk and angry man threatening
to kill my mom with a wicked swing of his arm.

At some point, I heard another bang, the front door thrown
open. Other, unfamiliar voices mingled with my dad's slurring,
loud diatribe. I heard shouting, but the door muffled everything. I couldn't make out anything, only anger and fear.

And then the door to my parents' room swung open and a policeman walked in, just like in a scene I might've watched on *Adam-12*. He walked over to the bed and I saw his full regalia — the baton, the gun at his side. I remember feeling relieved that the gun remained in his holster. *Okay, he doesn't have the gun out*, I thought. *That's a good thing.*

He leaned over me and put a hand on my chest. I imagine he just wanted to make sure I was still breathing. My eyes must've been as wide as saucers, and fear had practically paralyzed me for who knows how long. I could've looked dead.

"Are you all right?" he asked.

"Yeah," I remember saying. "I'm fine."

And you know the weird thing? I really was. The police had arrived. No one got hurt. I was too young to understand how that night would change my life forever, but my fists unclenched and I let go of the blanket. I was fine.

Dr. Dobson once talked to me about "resilience theory." Some children — perhaps 10 to 12 percent — suffer trauma and yet come out the other end relatively unscathed. These children can suffer unimaginable heartbreak and yet do just as well as if they had lived in Mayberry R.F.D. Maybe I fell into that category. Maybe God in his grace had given me the resilience I needed to deal with the traumas in my young life.

In any case, a switch flipped for me after the policeman walked in. No longer did I feel like a terrified little boy. I felt like a soldier, a figure from an old 1960s show called *Combat!* The policeman had walked out and shut the door behind him. I snuck out of the bed and crept to the door — crouched over to avoid imaginary enemy gunfire — and cracked the door open to spy on a scene that felt curiously distant from me.

The living room had emptied, but I heard voices in the front yard, through the open front door. So I made my way toward the front door, crouching, hiding behind bits of furniture, an imaginary gun in my hand. And finally, I peered through the open front door.

Two police cars sat in front of my house, their lights spinning and splashing the neighborhood in patriotic colors. My mom stood in the front yard. A policeman stood behind my dad, leading him away in handcuffs to a police car. My parents stared at each other as my dad shouted and screamed. They exchanged words and threats as the neighbors gathered to watch.

And there I stood in the doorway, watching it all as if it were a TV show. Behind me lay the warmth and security of home. Light from the empty house spilled onto the front yard in a neat rectangle, the shadow of a little boy cut out in the middle. The rest of the yard remained shrouded in darkness, occasionally washed by lights of red and blue.

Lifelong Impact

My life changed forever after that night. As I already noted, I saw my dad a little thereafter and even lived with him for a while. After some time, he started coming back to the house. He'd grab some food and say hello to any of the kids who happened to be there at the time.

But he never returned when my mom was around. The time between his quick visits grew and grew. Until I was eleven, my dad became an infrequent visitor to my life, a broken reed that might float by once in a while but never stayed, never making an impact on me or anyone else. In some ways, my dad — the father I had hoped for, the father I needed — vanished for good the night of the hammer.

Fathers need to be a lot of things — loving, strong, able

to set fair rules and consistently enforce them. A dad has a long roster of job requirements, and more always seems to get added to the list.

But before he can do anything else, a father has to *be there*. He has to be there physically. He has to be mentally present. He has to be emotionally available. He must be consistent. An inconsistent and unreliable father endangers his whole family. And while there may be many reasons that fathers wind up becoming an inconsistent, unreliable presence in their children's lives, no reason can fill the ensuing hole left in a child's heart.

But fathers who are committed to be present can make a difference that is too profound for words.

From what I hear and read, Rick van Beek has been there like few others for his daughter, Madison. Doctors diagnosed Madison with severe cerebral palsy about two months after her birth. About 75 percent of her brain doesn't function, and she operates at the level of a three-month-old infant. She wears diapers and is fed through a tube in her stomach. Maddy can't talk, walk, or see. But she can smile and laugh — and rarely had Rick seen Maddy so happy as when a friend pushed her in a racing stroller during Michigan's Grand Rapids Marathon several years ago.

"To see her being so happy and enjoying every bump in the road was more than I could handle," he wrote in a 2010 blog post.[26]

After seeing his daughter so enthralled with running in 2008, Rick dropped his two-pack-a-day smoking habit and began to train for marathons, triathlons, and anything else he felt Maddy might enjoy. The triathlons (in which competitors must swim, bike, and run) present perhaps the greatest challenge. For the swimming portion, Rick tows Maddy in a kayak. She rides in a special cart behind Rick's bike in the second leg of the event, and Rick pushes her in a stroller for the final stretch. During each transition, Rick must carry Maddy to the next apparatus and strap her in safely — transitions made all the more difficult because of the stabilizing steel rods fused to Madison's spine.

As of 2012, Rick and Madison had completed seventy-five events together.

"I've never once heard my daughter say 'I love you,' say 'thank you,' or 'I need this' or 'I need that' or anything," Rick says on his video blog.[27] "But when she's in her cart running with me, riding behind me in the bike, sitting in the kayak when we're swimming, it doesn't matter. The smile on her face is all that I need to make it worthwhile."

"I'm not running this race," Rick adds. "Madison is running this race. Maddy. Team Maddy. We're not racing. We're conquering everything that has held us back."

Rick and Maddy's remarkable story can feel intimidating to some. Few of us will face the sort of challenges confronting the van Beek family. Few of us will try to carry our children as we compete in triathlons.

But all of us will have to carry them through rough spots and dark patches. We'll be asked to share the good times and bad times with them. We'll need to provide the stabilization, the oak at their back, that they need so much.

"I'm a man," Rick says. "I've got big shoulders ... I can handle it. I'm ready to go."[28]

We all should be ready to go. We all should provide the kind of consistent presence in our children's lives that will help them travel farther than they ever thought possible. Our kids need that from us. They deserve it from us. And we should reassure them that, whatever twists and turns or bumps and dips come, we'll always be there with them.

TO THINK ABOUT

1. Did you have an inconsistent father? Can you remember a moment when you needed him and he wasn't there for you? How did that failure affect you?

2. Have you ever been exposed to abuse or a domestic violence situation? Did the experience change you?

3. Have you ever been an inconsistent father? What happened? Did you find a way to make it up to your child?

4. Which is worse — to be physically absent, like an out-of-the-picture, "deadbeat" dad, or to be someone who's there but is unreliable, like my father?

5. What steps can you take to become a more consistent, more reliable father?

Seven

The Promise of Time

I ADJUSTED TO LIFE WITHOUT DAD. MY HOME LIFE REMAINED a mess, but I began to find my place on the playground. I loved sports, and by the age of six, I already saw myself (and other kids saw me) as something of an athlete. At recess, I'd pick the teams. Here, at last, I had found one area of my life where I felt *good*. Sports became my sanctuary, and I loved playing them, particularly baseball, more than almost anything else at that time.

In the middle of July, just days away from my seventh birthday, I walked into the kitchen and found my father rummaging through the fridge.

"Dad!" I said. I hadn't seen him in months. "What're you doing?"

"Oh, I just came by to pick up something to eat," he answered.

I don't think he expected to see me. To this day I wonder how often he came by just to grab some food, leaving before anyone saw him there.

But in the moment, I didn't think about the food he took. I

didn't think about the hammer or the pool. I didn't think about anything other than the fact that Dad, *my* dad, had come home to see me again. My heart almost pounded out of my chest, and I couldn't stop smiling.

And better yet, my dad smiled back. He might not have expected to see me, but he seemed glad at the sight. At least, so thought the almost-seven-year-old me.

"My birthday's coming up!" I blurted.

"Is it?" my dad replied. And he paused for a second. "What do you want for your birthday?" he asked.

I shrugged my shoulders.

"Tell you what," he said, leaning in a little closer. "Why don't I bring you a mitt? A real leather one."

If I had felt excited before, that was nothing compared to how I felt right then. The fractured Daly family didn't exactly swim in cash. We didn't have a lot of stuff, and a leather mitt would've been on a par with getting a PlayStation 4 today.

But considering my love of baseball, the promise seemed exponentially greater. A mitt! A leather mitt! It was as if my dad had read my mind and saw, not just a great gift, but the *perfect* one. I needed a mitt. I knew I'd use it every day during the summer. It'd make a huge difference for me on the base-ball diamond, snagging grounders and tracking down fly balls. And each time a baseball hit the pocket with a soft *thwap*, maybe part of me would think of my dad and how he loved me enough to give me such a great present.

It was almost too good to be true. I nodded my head like a little wild man and smiled fiercely.

"Well, all right then," he said. "I'll come by on your birthday with your mitt." And he left.

Leading up to my birthday party, I could think of nothing but that mitt. I imagined how it'd feel as I slid it on my hand, the rich smell of the leather, the sound it'd make when I'd thump my fist in the pocket. All my friends would want to try it on. They'd tell me how cool it was. I'd feel so proud of the glove. "My dad gave it to me," I'd tell them. Imagining it all, it almost felt like a return to the days when Dad delivered doughnuts for a living and he seemed like the coolest guy in the world.

Before he ran around smashing the house with a hammer.

So when my birthday finally came, one of the first things I did was run out to the curb and wait for my dad to arrive with his promised present. When he didn't come right away, I wasn't too worried. It was still early in the day. I knew he'd arrive sometime. He'd come. Surely when my birthday party got in full swing, he'd come.

"My dad's bringing me a mitt," I told my friend Ricky during my birthday party. And Ricky, good friend that he was, seemed almost as excited as me. We ran out to the curb together and looked up and down Sixth Street in Alhambra, California. We knew that pretty soon we'd see a familiar person walking down the road toward us. And I could feel in my heart the moment he would walk up to me, my mitt in his hand, and give it to me — along with a big hug. I kept looking up and down the sidewalk for him.

We probably ran out to the curb and back a dozen times that afternoon. But as the day wore on, the hope began to dwindle and the anticipation began to feel more like desperation. *My dad'll come*, I thought. *He's coming with the mitt. He promised.*

As the sun edged toward the western horizon, Ricky went home. "Call me when he comes," he said — but I think by then, Ricky knew the truth. I think he caught on long before I did.

As Ricky walked away, I felt the sting of embarrassment. My dad didn't even think enough of me to keep his promise.

Promises, Promises

I didn't see my father again for years. And while it may sound harsh, I don't think I even really wanted to. I still loved him, but that afternoon, something snapped. I was done. Finished. For me, the baseball mitt — on the heels of my experience at the pool and the night he brought the hammer home — took me out emotionally. Maybe I'd been unfair. Maybe I shouldn't have put my dad on a "three strikes and you're out" policy. But I was seven years old, not old enough to think about my dad's problems and how his alcoholism might've impacted his ability to be a good father. I was in no position to be fair. I knew only that he couldn't be trusted. He couldn't keep his promises.

Broken promises are a big deal, especially to a child. As parents, we remind our kids of the importance of keeping their word. We tell them not to lie. We expect them to follow through on what they say they're going to do. And our children, rightly, expect the very same from us.

That's why this story — about me, my dad, and the baseball mitt I never got — hits people in a way that nothing else does. It feels so *familiar*. Not many folks know what it feels like to have their dad go after their mom. But almost everybody knows what a broken promise feels like. Almost every time I finish speaking, people, men especially, come up to me blinking back tears. Often they're teens. Sometimes they're grown men. But almost all say, essentially, the same thing: "You know, that was *my* dad."

When our parents break a promise, we remember it forever. I came out of a childhood in which my father broke *a lot* of promises. And those broken promises wound up making it difficult for me to trust anyone. A father's untrustworthiness, of course, impacts far more than a child's trust.

Experts say that how you handle promises can teach your children about the importance of integrity, honesty, and respect. This integrity says a lot about you, how you can be counted on to mean what you say. The honesty gets reflected in the word you keep; you say what you mean. And you show respect by honoring the promise you made to another person, particularly if that person is your son or daughter. When you keep your word, it tells them not only that the promise itself is important but that *they're* important. It marks you as a person who loves them, a person they can depend on.

But when that promise gets broken, your kids receive a very different message — that they're less important than whatever made you break your promise, be it a day at work or a night of drinking. A broken promise makes the child feel unworthy. Less. Diminished.

Keeping his word to his children is one of the most important things a father can do. And the Bible, I believe, backs me up.

God, our heavenly Father, made many promises to his children. And he has always been as good as his word, in both the Old and New Testaments. "Praise be to the LORD, who has given rest to his people Israel just as he promised," we read in 1 Kings 8:56. "Not one word has failed of all the good promises he gave through his servant Moses." And in 2 Corinthians 1:20–22, Paul writes, "For no matter how many promises God has made, they are 'Yes' in Christ. And so through him the 'Amen' is spoken by us to the glory of God. Now it is God who makes both us and you stand firm in Christ. He anointed us, set his seal of ownership on us, and put his Spirit in our hearts as a deposit, guaranteeing what is to come."

God's promises form the foundation of our faith. Without those promises, we build our church on shifting sand. We trust God because he has proven trustworthy. And since the family itself mirrors in many ways our own relationship with our Creator, keeping our promises as dads becomes almost a sacred duty. "All you need to say is simply 'Yes' or 'No,'" Jesus tells us in Matthew 5:37. "Anything beyond this comes from the evil one." And when we don't follow through on our "yes" and "no," we fall short of being the dads God wants us to be.

My own kids know that keeping my promises is a central creed with me. In the Daly household, that means two things.

First, I'm wary of making promises I'm not sure I can keep. I'm very cautious in my vocabulary, making a strong distinction between a *promise* and a *maybe*. If I'd like to take Trent and Troy to a ball game but work's a little crazy, I'll say, "That's a maybe. We might be able to go, but I'm not sure. I'll let you know as soon as I can." And if I *do* make a promise, I try to make sure that nothing short of fire, flood, or earthquake will block me from keeping it.

Second, when I make a promise, I rely on my boys to hold me accountable. When your kids are about the same ages as mine are right now, you have to be careful of hypocrisy. Trent and Troy are inching closer to adulthood themselves, and so naturally they watch very carefully the adults around them. They learn, by watching, how adults act and react. *Are they trustworthy? Can I count on them?* And if they see hypocrisy in me or in another adult, particularly as it comes to expression in broken promises, that fault will hinder the relationship. A big enough broken promise might even break the relationship.

I try to reinforce with my boys the idea that I don't break promises. Once each month or so, I'll ask Trent and Troy,

"Have I done a good job of keeping my promises to you?" and they'll say, "Yeah!" Then I'll ask, "Have I broken any?" And I hope they'll answer, "No!"

These conversations keep me accountable. When I ask those questions, I mean them sincerely, and I want a sincere answer.

But as strange as it might sound at first, there's also an element of branding in those questions.

Let me explain. We sometimes talk about fatherhood as a job without realizing that it's more than a cliché. In many respects it *is* a job—it may not pay much, but the pension plan comes packed with love and hugs. And your children are, in a way, your customers. You can do things to reinforce your "brand" as a father—the kinds of things that any business does. If you tell your customers "you're number one; we're all about you" and you don't answer the phone or you respond harshly when someone wants to return an item, it doesn't jibe. The same goes with your children. If you say, "I love you," and you don't show them your love, it won't take long for your kids to figure out something's wrong. If you tell your children that promises matter and then you break your own promises, they'll realize very quickly that, not only can they not trust you, but the lessons you're trying to teach seem pointless.

When I first started asking my sons about whether I've done a good job of keeping my promises, I wasn't only asking them to hold me accountable. I wanted to instill an idea about how I wanted them to see me as a father. And now, every time I ask them whether I've broken a promise, as long as they say no, that reinforces my "brand" as an honest and trustworthy dad. I work hard at never breaking a promise. And by talking about it with them, I make sure they understand not only the importance of keeping promises. I want them to see that I keep *my* promises. I want them to remember it, almost top of mind. There may come a time when Trent or Troy, in their mid-teens, won't instinctively look up to me like they do now. But maybe through my branding strategy, they'll still know I'm in their corner. When they're fifteen or sixteen, I might not look as cool as I do today. They may consider me an annoying bother or a pain in the rear. But they'll remember that I keep my promises, no matter what. They can trust me to do what I said I would do. When everything else grows uncertain, I want this to remain a truth they can bank on: *Dad keeps his promises.*

We should always be held accountable to keep our word. Since promises are easy to make and easy to break, we ought to make *our* promises very hard to break.

I'd Die for You

We men are big talkers. When we get married, we tell our spouses, "I'll do anything for you" — and we mean it … at the time. When our kids are born, we'll say, "I'll die for you" — and we're not lying when we say it. We love those grandiose promises. They sound so … *impressive.* They feed our sense of being the family hero — the brave and fearless soldier, the storybook character who'll run into a burning building to rescue kids and cats and photo albums.

I'd love to see the statistics of how many people ever get in a position to actually fulfill those massive sacrificial promises. How many men ever get asked to, literally, die for their wives or kids in this society? One in a thousand? Ten thousand? A hundred thousand? It's not many, I can guarantee you that. Even when we make heartfelt pledges, in some ways they're the easiest of all promises to make, because the likelihood of someone ever needing to cash in that promissory chip is so remote. And eventually, the people in our lives figure it out. *You'll die for me*, our wives will think, *but you won't do what I need you to do this evening at home. You say you'll do anything for me, but you won't run to the grocery store and pick up some milk. You'll sacrifice everything, but you won't sacrifice the three minutes required to take out the trash.*

It's not the big promises that make a real difference in the family, but the small ones. The promise you make to your son to help him build a birdhouse. The promise you make to your daughter to quiz her on her math fundamentals. The promise to play *Monopoly* or *Uno* Thursday after dinner or take the kids to a movie on Saturday afternoon.

"I'll die for you," we tell our children. "That's great," they answer back, "but can I just spend time with you?"

Taking the Time

We struggle to keep our promises in large part because they almost always require our most precious commodity — time. And yet time is what our kids want from us more than anything. We don't win their affection through somber life lessons or shiny new bicycles. They don't need our presents. They need our presence. As much as I would've treasured that baseball mitt my dad never gave me, I wanted so much more — an afternoon with him to break it in, a few precious hours to throw a baseball to me and let me catch it.

Our promises become the battleground where our heroic ambitions run smack into our selfish natures. We love our kids, but we love our time too. And we get protective of the little time we have.

Our lives move at an incredibly fast pace. Our work

demands so much from us. Our diversions have never diverted us more. These things take away time we could be spending with our children, which means we must intentionally carve out an hour or two to spend with the kids. But often, we struggle with making that sort of sacrifice for the sake of our children. All adults can act selfishly in that way, and I think especially dads can do so. It's all about our time: *I don't want to do that right now. I don't want to pick that up now. I'm not going to play that now. I'm going to watch the news. I'm going to watch the game. Don't tell me what to do.*

I see this selfishness in myself, particularly during football season. After we get home from church, I could easily sit and watch three NFL games, one right after the other. And I don't even have cable! If I had the NFL RedZone channel, Jean and the kids might never see me. I love watching football. Just *love* it. And I have to rein in that love as best I can for the sake of my family. It's not easy, but I do my best.

We all can feel pulled away from the family by the fun distractions of life. We dads work hard. Many of us labor more than forty hours a week to provide for our wives and kids. We get called to do other worthwhile duties outside of work — helping out at church, serving on our neighborhood watch committees, coaching baseball. We relish our downtime. Frankly, we deserve some.

And here's a little secret you won't hear in most fatherhood books. Spending time with kids, particularly very young kids, can feel like work. It doesn't necessarily come naturally.

Oh, you can have some wonderful times with your children, moments you'll treasure and remember forever. And the more time you devote to your children, the easier those moments will come. But obviously you and your kids are at very different stages of your lives. Your kids don't laugh at your jokes and couldn't care less about hearing how your day at work went. We dads don't always feel terribly interested in getting a twenty-minute recap of how David laughed so hard at lunch that milk came out his nose. Maybe they don't understand why you want to watch football. You sure don't get their love of *The Wiggles*. If men are from Mars and women are from Venus, sometimes it seems like kids come from Alpha Centauri.

Mothers seem to know instinctively how to relate to little children. Their God-given ability to nurture swings into gear. Then as the kids get older and enter their tweens and teens, fathers feel more equipped to engage. But until the kids get to that point, dads can feel a little clueless with their little ones. They don't know what to say or do or how to interact. Some fathers can feel downright afraid of spending time with their four-year-old. And this fear can make it all the more difficult to devote to the child the time he or she needs.

I was in the same boat. I felt awkward around our boys in their younger years. I just didn't know how to relate. And guys, we bond while doing *something*. We work on cars. We build fences. We play golf. We play basketball. That's how we typically build relationships with each other. We don't sit around on the sofa and talk about stuff. We're action oriented. But little kids don't really do much. And when our kids can't do action with us, we feel lost.

But we have to get over that feeling. When we say to our family, "I would do anything for you," we have to mean it. Because "anything" sometimes means getting uncomfortable and feeling a little lost. It might mean watching *The Wiggles* with your son or sipping pretend tea with your daughter. This isn't about us and the fifty work-related things we're thinking about or the football game we're missing. It's about *them* — our kids. Maybe we don't want to do it all the time. But we should do it. We have to become less selfish. We have to become more sacrificial.

"I would die for you," we tell our kids. Guess what? We actually have the chance to die a little every day. We can die to ourselves and to our selfish wants. We can sacrifice our time and energy for the sake of our children. Just as Christ died for us, we can die for our families — perhaps not literally, but in ways that'll actually mean a lot more to our kids as time goes on. It may surprise you to see the dividends a little bit of time can pay.

What Does That Time Look Like?

It gets better, of course. It gets easier and more rewarding to spend time with your children. But to get to a level of comfort, it takes some time. Just as your children need those hours with you to feel appreciated, so you need to spend those hours with them to learn how to become a better father. Your kids don't come with instruction manuals. There is no easy template to follow to raise them well. Each child is a little different and often will require a different part of you.

My boys are a great example of this. Troy is very physically affectionate. He thrives on physical touch. On some lazy mornings, he'll just hop into our bed and lay his head on my chest and wriggle right into me, like a puppy. "I love you, Daddy," he'll say. He shows his love for me through that physicality, and so I show it to him in the same way. He wants a hug. He wants me to run my fingers through his hair, just like I needed and wanted from my own father.

Trent doesn't need as much physical attention. I hug him because I want him to appreciate it and remember it, but he doesn't need it. More than anything, he needs my energy and attention. He needs me to tell him he's okay, to express some words of affirmation because sometimes he can feel a little insecure. His self-worth is often at risk because he doesn't feel like he measures up. I'm often a calming influence in his life. I can settle him down when he gets frustrated. When he and his mom go at it, I can serve as his confidant. And so I have to modify my mode of parenting to fit his needs.

Troy needs to feel my touch. Trent needs to hear what I have to say. I figured out what my boys most need from their dad only by spending time with them.

So much of parenthood is about being aware, about observing what your children need. You have to get in tune with your child and become a student of him or her. You study them. You learn how they act when something bothers them. When they get excited about something. Even when they hide something. It's like sailing a boat, knowing instinctively what to do when the wind turns and the waves begin to curl a certain way. Or like a ballroom dancer, who after years of dancing with the same partner knows how to complement each lift of the foot or twist of the head. Or a quarterback with his teammates who senses when the tight end's going to break and how quickly the wideout can make it twenty yards downfield. You're in control because you know the players.

Fathers have to know their players. They need to become sensitive to what their kids do well and where they struggle, when to lend a hand and when to let them loose. No parenting book or website will tell you how to do these things. It comes only with time and attention.

And that time and attention will pay huge dividends, I promise you.

A Most Precious Gift

Christian comedian Ken Davis tells of a man who went fishing with his son. After spending all day at the lake without getting a nibble, the two of them finally went home.

Years later, the man rummaged through some old boxes and found two journals — one he had written in when his son was young and the other written in by the son. He opened the journals to the entry for the day they had gone fishing together.

His own journal entry read, "Didn't catch a thing. A whole day wasted."

His son's journal had quite a different take. "Spent the whole day with my dad — greatest day of my life."

Time is indeed our most valuable resource. We can't waste what little we're given. But our children consider time no less precious than we do. And when we give it to them, they understand what a precious gift it is.

Few people gave me that gift when I was a boy. I felt very alone for much of my childhood. My father loved me, but he rarely spent time with me. Hank couldn't be bothered. And my older brothers and sisters and I didn't have much in common. They saw me as the typical annoying little brother, always making a nuisance of himself. I wanted to hang out with my brothers and sisters, but I wasn't a teenager. I couldn't do the sort of things they did. I got lost in the shuffle.

For a while, my oldest brother, Mike, probably represented the closest thing I had to a father figure, mainly because of his physical stature. He was a big guy, six foot five, and a rock — a college football player, a tough sailor in the Navy, the whole bit. And while we've grown quite close now, we never hung out while growing up. The ten-year age difference was just too big to overcome.

I used to look forward to his shore leave when Mike would come home to Long Beach, California. But before long, the reality of his visits sank in. A nineteen-year-old didn't want to hang out with his nine-year-old brother. When he came home, I'd get a hug. "It's good to see you, Jim," he'd say. And then he'd leave again, to hang out and party with his friends.

But I remember one noteworthy exception.

When Mike's ship came in, Mike often invited a lot of his Navy pals to the house — mainly, I think, so they could spend time at a house. During one long weekend leave, he invited about twenty guys to come over.

Most of them tried to be nice to me — at least as nice as Navy guys can manage to act around a nine-year-old tagalong. One afternoon, I followed them to the park, where we all played football. And when I say "we," I really mean "they." Sometimes they'd rotate me in and let me play, slinging the football in my direction and tackling me gently. They were awfully nice about it, but at the time it ticked me off. I knew they were patronizing me, not taking me seriously at all. They ignored me, in a gentle way. And that really annoyed me, because I thought I was better than half of 'em. If this nine-year-old boy tended to get lost in the middle of his four brothers and sisters, I felt *really* lost with a flock of Navy guys.

But one of Mike's friends, a guy named Russell Boles, took some time out for me. While the rest of the guys returned to the park or spent time downtown or flirted with my sisters, Russell stayed with me at the house. We built a model together one day, a 1967 Pontiac GTO. We glued it together and painted it, just me and him. It took all day.

He just hung out with me. Even with all his buddies there, he chose to hang out with me. It was the coolest thing *ever*.

I don't know why Russell Boles gave me that precious gift

of time. Maybe he had a younger brother he missed back home in Kansas. Maybe I reminded him of himself as a boy. I don't know. But whatever the reason, I'm grateful for it. More than forty years later, I still remember and treasure that day. I still remember Russell Boles, the only guy who ever really gave me, in my early years, the gift of time.

Now, if a total stranger can have that kind of positive impact in a boy's life and be remembered so fondly for so long afterward, how much more of an impact can you as a dad have on your child's well-being? How much more will your children treasure the time you spend with them?

Clark Miller, a good friend and former coworker, once gave me a great piece of advice about raising children. "Try to say yes as often as you can," he told me. But to say yes to your children often means saying no to something you'd like to do. It often means taking time out for them. Sometimes it means making a promise. Those two things often go hand in hand.

I'm guilty of often saying no. But to say yes — that's a beautiful thing.

The Power of Promise

Just before I turned seven, my father promised me a glove but never delivered. I've never forgotten that broken promise.

Maybe he didn't either.

Four years later, I began living with my dad again. The weirdness of the Reils was just barely in the rear-view mirror. I was eleven years old. My father was trying to get sober. And it felt as though we both had a chance at a fresh start.

As a way to celebrate this new beginning, my dad asked me if I'd like to go to a Los Angeles Dodgers baseball game.

Would I? Was that a trick question?

The Dodgers, as any baseball-crazy kid knew, were playing a doubleheader that day against the Cincinnati Reds, maybe one of the best baseball teams ever. They were known as the Big Red Machine back then and had a roster packed with future Hall of Famers. The Dodgers, who made three World Series appearances in the 1970s, weren't too shabby either. This was *the* baseball rivalry at the time. You couldn't find a hotter ticket in town.

Even better, I'd attend the game with my dad, a man who loved baseball as much as I did. He never played catch with me as a kid. Never taught me to hit. But there, in Dodgers Stadium, we could still bond over the game we both loved. The game that, maybe indirectly, my dad taught me to love.

Dad didn't own a car at the time, and Dodger Stadium was probably close to twenty miles away. We had to take the bus, and the last one would leave for the stadium at about four thirty. That would get us to the stadium in time for warm-ups. It was already about four o'clock, so we knew we were cutting it a little close. Dad told me to get ready as quickly as I could. And I did. We dashed out the door and skittered over to the bus stop, just as the bus to Dodger Stadium pulled away.

"We're never going to get there in time," I said. And just like that, it felt like the same story all over again: An afternoon with my dad, vanishing in a haze of bus exhaust. Another promise broken.

But my dad didn't blink. Before the bus got out of sight, he flagged down a cab, and we hopped in, cruising to the game in almost unimaginable luxury. Just days before, I had escaped the craziness of the Reils, remember, so to be going to the game with my father — my real father — felt almost too good to be true.

It really was a magical afternoon and evening. We wound

up getting there early, and I got a baseball signed by some of the all-time greats of the 1970s who played for the teams — Johnny Bench, Joe Morgan, and Pete Rose for the Reds; Steve Garvey and Davey Lopes for the Dodgers. Two of them, Morgan and Bench, are in the Hall of Fame. If I still had the ball today, it'd be worth about seven grand. Unfortunately, like a stupid kid, I used it to play a pickup game the next day, and by the time we got through with it, so much dirt and tar covered it that you couldn't even read most of the names.

But you know what? That's okay. Because when I look back on that day, I don't think much about the games or the scores or even that Hall of Fame baseball. I think of my dad flagging down that cab without a second thought. He made probably just a couple hundred bucks a week back then, and he spent about half that on the cab ride. It was a huge sacrifice for him. But he had told me we were going to the game. He had promised, and this was one promise he intended to keep.

That's one of my fondest memories of my father. He spent time with me. He sacrificed for me. He kept his promise.

When a father breaks a promise, kids remember it forever. But you know what? When they *keep* a promise, they remember *that* forever too.

——————— TO THINK ABOUT ———————

1. What promises did your dad make to you when you were a child? Can you remember ones that he kept? Ones that he broke?

2. If you have children, how do you like to spend time with them? What sorts of things do you like to do? How could you make even more time for them?

3. The chapter advises, "Try to say yes as often as you can." How often do you say yes to your children? Are you sometimes selfish with your time?

4. How can you introduce your children to your own interests — things like golf or football or working on cars? How willing have you been to learn to appreciate what interests them?

5. Do you find that your kids need different versions of "Dad"? If so, how can you show a unique father touch to each of your children?

Eight

Learning and Living Together

Not long ago, a Christian speaker admitted to his audience that his son was in prison for burglary.

"But," he said, "we've done a great job as parents." The crowd looked puzzled. "Because actually," he added, "he was born an ax murderer."

Naturally, the audience laughed. It's a great line. There's absolutely no truth in it, but it's a great line. And in its own weird way, it hits the heart of what we're supposed to be doing as parents — showing and telling our kids how to become good, reliable, upstanding adults, and as we do so, gently guiding them away from the serial killer career track.

Parents are teachers. And from the day our kids are born, we're on the job. Sometimes we don't even know that we're teaching. Our kids learn how to smile and laugh and talk simply by watching and listening to us, and they figure out quickly that screaming is a *great* way to get some attention. And as they grow up, they continue to learn from us by observation, often regretfully so. Kids who unexpectedly start cussing in front of Grandma may have picked up those choice words from Daddy during a particularly stressful drive to school. Statistically, teens who become smokers or drinkers took their first cues from Mom and Dad. The old cliché of "do as I say, not as I do"? Children hardly ever listen to that piece of advice.

But often, we do give our kids *very* intentional lessons. We encourage them to walk and show them how to use the potty by themselves (in the appropriate receptacle, we hope). We teach them to always tell the truth and to look both ways before crossing the street. We train them how to hold their silverware correctly and how to use a stick shift.

But I believe we have a more fundamental and basic lesson to teach our kids. We must teach them what reality is. We must show them how to look at the world with a clear eye and sober heart. We have to show them that, while beauty may be in the eye of the beholder, truth isn't. Truth remains the same wherever one finds it. And a key to growing up on this planet reasonably healthy and happy is to recognize the truth when we see it.

It's a trickier proposition than you might think, particularly in our confusing twenty-first century. Lots of people out there today tell us that truth is really a matter of opinion — "You have your truth, I have mine." Spin obscures everything, from advertising pitches and marketing gimmicks to political punditry and sophistry. Plenty of people out there try to convince us that up is down (or at least a little crooked or slanted). Our own emotions and biases can obscure the real truth, and so we have to teach our sons and daughters how to look past what they feel in the moment and see the bigger picture.

Of course, for us dads to teach the truth to our kids, we have to know it ourselves. And that's where we often struggle.

After all, we have our own emotions and biases to contend with. We have our own susceptibilities to spin. And sometimes our take on the world might be just plain off.

If our kids got locked away for burglary, we might very much want to believe that our good parenting saved them from an even worse fate. But the truth might look a lot different.

Reality at the Reils'

My time with the Reil family might rank as the most surreal period in my life. *Everything* about my time there strikes me as odd. In fairness to the Reils, I arrived when I was nine and reeling from an overload of turmoil. I recognize that they stepped up when we needed help, and for that, I am grateful.

But even the house seemed odd. It probably didn't measure more than twelve hundred square feet, but the Reils had a big family. Sometimes ten to twelve people could be living there at once — six Reils, three of us Dalys, and sometimes two or three others. And it seemed the Reils' huge kitchen table took up half the house. No matter how big their household grew, everyone could sit around the thing.

How they passed the time seemed odd. They spent hours around that monstrous table rolling cigarettes, using a huge cigarette machine and a tub of tobacco. They'd open up the machine and put in a filter, a sheet of cigarette paper, and a sprinkle of tobacco. After they closed it, the machine rolled everything together, went *pa-ching*, and they had a nicely rolled cigarette. Because the Reils didn't have a television, they spent their mornings and evenings in the kitchen, listening to AM radio and rolling cigarettes. *Pa-ching! Pa-ching!*

Even our rare moments of fun at the Reils' seemed odd (partly the fault of my brother, Dave). Every once in a while, just to break the monotony, Dave would put on some old army boots, don a hospital gown (exposing his butt), color out a tooth, and dance to his own rendition of "Orange Blossom Special." I don't think I ever heard laughter in that strange small house except when my brother wiggled his rear to "Orange Blossom Special."

But nothing could top the odd behavior of the Reils themselves. Granted, Kevin, their eighteen-year-old son, seemed very kind and cool, the kind of guy you wanted to grow up and be like. But he and my brother hung out together and didn't stick around the house much.

Dale, Mr. Reil's nineteen-year-old son, married his forty-two-year-old cousin (so I was told). Steve, fifteen, would barricade himself in the bathroom and threaten to swallow a bottle of aspirin whenever he got upset. Years later, someone told me he had become a homosexual activist in San Francisco and died of HIV/AIDS in the early 1980s. Ben stole my toys and put them in his drawer. And Mr. Reil? Well, I knew the moment I met him that he was a little off. But nothing prepared me for what happened when a social worker came around to see how Dave, Dee Dee, and I had settled in.

Wrongly Accused

The social worker, a very nice woman in her late twenties, visited the home about six months into our stay and sat down with Dave and me at the kitchen table. She'd already had a chat with Mr. and Mrs. Reil, and I vaguely wondered what she must've thought of the Reils and their homestead, with the huge dining room table in the living room, the cigarette machine in the kitchen, and the chickens and rabbits out back.

And I admit that I secretly hoped the social worker had found a more normal home for Dave, Dee Dee, and me.

So my heart leaped a little when she looked in our eyes and said, "Look, I think we have a problem." But the pregnant pause after she spoke made me edgy again.

She lowered her voice. "Mr. Reil said that you tried to kill him."

I felt shocked. *Dave would never try to kill anybody*, I thought. I knew him better than anyone, and he had no killer anywhere in him. Sure, he'd had his share of fights. But I never saw anything like that between him and Mr. Reil. I figured we had a serious misunderstanding at work here.

"Dave?" I said incredulously, turning to him.

"No, Jimmy," the social worker said gently. "Mr. Reil claims *you* tried to kill him."

If I had felt shock before, words can't describe how I felt now.

"*Me?*" I said.

"Jimmy?" Dave asked.

She nodded.

"But — I'm ten years old!"

Sure, I felt miserable at the Reils'. Of all the rocky times I experienced in my childhood, the year I spent with them ranked as the most difficult. Home, which should be a place of refuge for children, had become a place of near terror for me. I dreaded the end of each school day. When I walked home, part of me hoped I could just keep walking forever, that I'd never have to turn down the street to the Reils' awful house. Yes, I felt lonely there. Helpless. And yes, some kids, I suppose, might've lashed out in a place like that — yelled or screamed or pushed back.

But I didn't. That just wasn't me. I didn't want to hurt anybody. I just wanted to curl in on myself. I just wanted to keep quiet, do my chores, and stay out of everybody's way. I wanted to disappear, stay unnoticed. The thought of harming anyone never crossed my mind, even as a fantasy.

But I felt pretty sure it didn't matter. Accused of attempted murder? Sure, she'd believe it. After all, the Reils refused to believe me when I told them Ben was stealing my stuff. So why would a social worker stick up for me with the Reils? They were my guardians, after all. Everyone would believe them over a ten-year-old kid.

And so I wondered, *Would she call the police or take me away in handcuffs? Would I go to jail? Did they even have jails for little kids?*

All that raced through my mind as I sat and stared at the social worker. And then, suddenly, a smile swept across her face — a kind, gentle smile — and I could breathe again. The smile told me I wouldn't go to jail. That she knew I wasn't the sort of ten-year-old who'd try to kill his foster father.

"How?" I blurted.

"Mr. Reil claims you tried to push him off a cliff," she said.

Wow, this story just gets weirder and weirder, I thought. We lived in the middle of the *desert*, with no cliffs for miles. Sure, we had a shallow ravine out back, but it was hardly a life-threatening precipice.

Mr. Reil was so convinced I intended to murder him that for some time he'd taken to sleeping in the rabbit hutch. I don't know whether he thought I wouldn't find him out there or that I couldn't sneak out to the hutch without him noticing, or maybe he thought the rabbits might offer him some protection — a cadre of fluffy bodyguards. Considering how many rabbits we ate for dinner, you'd think he would've had more to fear from *them* than from me.

As I look back on that year, I'm sure it was difficult for their family too. We disrupted their home and lives. I greatly admire foster parents and the sacrifice they make to help children. When a foster home helps carry the rocks, however, it has to make sure it doesn't add to the bag.

The social worker promised to have a little talk with Mr. Reil, and she said if we felt uncomfortable there, we could get funneled back into the foster care system and hope for other families that might provide a better match. But it would mean Dave, Dee Dee, and I would likely get split up — and that thought terrified me more than an unhinged foster father.

After all, I'd grown used to bad dads. I couldn't trust my real dad to make wise decisions for his family. I couldn't trust my stepfather, Hank, to stick around when things got tough. And Mr. Reil? I couldn't trust him even to know reality. And since my luck got progressively worse with each father figure, I thought we ought to just stick together and get through it at the Reils'.

From then on, I didn't feel love or fear or even anger for Mr. Reil. I felt pity. Pity that I, a little boy of ten, had a better grasp on reality than he did.

Get Real

My experience with Mr. Reil is an extreme example of not knowing reality. Most of us don't suffer from such extreme delusion, and few of us fathers conjure up imaginary dangers so severe that we hide in rabbit hutches.

But all of us can shut our eyes to the things that go on

around us. And as fathers, we need to do the best job possible to know reality — not as we'd like it to be or fear it to be, but as it really is.

Jesus addressed that sense of reality in Matthew 7:3 – 5: "Why do you look at the speck of sawdust in your brother's eye and pay no attention to the plank in your own eye? How can you say to your brother, 'Let me take the speck out of your eye,' when all the time there is a plank in your own eye? You hypocrite, first take the plank out of your own eye, and then you will see clearly to remove the speck from your brother's eye."

In a sense, Jesus asked us, "Do you know reality? Not what you *think* you see, not what you *think* you feel. Do you know what is real?"

As fathers, we need to know reality. We must know how others see us. How we really speak to others. The difference between fact and opinion.

We need to, for instance, be real in how we see ourselves and our own strengths and weaknesses. Where have we come up short in raising a family? When have we failed to spend time with our wives and kids? How do our shortcomings affect those around us? We have to be honest with ourselves, because only then can we be honest with our children. We need to apologize when we do something wrong and make it up to them the best way we know how.

We need to be honest about our own children too. Sometimes we believe our kids can do no wrong, and so when a teacher calls to tell us that little Johnny is acting out in class or isn't paying attention during social studies, we blame the teacher. Some parents see the opposite when it comes to their children — that they can never get anything right. We scold and chastise them for every little thing until we crush their spirit and bring their tether to us nearly to its breaking point.

And, most importantly, we need to get on the same page with Mom, our child-rearing partner.

Father — and Mother — Know Best Together

Here we come to another "trickier than it sounds" challenge, because more often than not, moms and dads have very different ideas of what's really going on.

Imagine you and your wife are looking at a big modern sculpture, but you don't get a chance to walk around and see the whole thing. You look at it from one angle, and your spouse views it from an entirely different angle. Once you get back together and talk it over, you have a better chance of figuring out what the sculpture really looked like, because together you saw more of it than either of you did alone.

But what if you got together and disagreed with what each other saw? You saw a long, thin, yellow sculpture, and so your wife's testimony that she saw something green that bowed in the middle strikes you as preposterous. And your wife, who knows *exactly* what she saw, can't believe you would doubt her, particularly when any idiot can see the thing is *green*. "You're wrong," you both say to the other. And then you both cross your arms and yell at each other, trying to prove how wrong your spouse is.

Sometimes our reality gets confused by our perspective. And when someone else, even our spouse, offers a different perspective, we can find it hard to accept. It gets even trickier when the reality involves one of us. A lot of couples have trouble figuring out reality. Mom has a very different perception about Dad's failures, and Dad has a very different perception of Mom's failures.

Not long ago, I got home from a trip and noticed that Jean

had hung a note on our refrigerator door. "Trent owes $6 for what he bought at the Dollar Store." I didn't think much of it, and I went about my business.

The next morning, as I got ready, Jean gave me instructions on what the kids would need to do when everyone got home. And then, out of the blue, she wheeled around and said, "And don't give them any money if they're out and want to buy something!"

I was a little taken aback. "Okay," I said, feeling defensive and wondering, *When did I last give them money for anything?*

"I mean it," she said. "And don't believe it if they tell you they have money at the house either."

And then I remembered the note.

"Wait a minute," I said. "Is this about the Dollar Store? Did you just do that? Did you just give Trent six bucks?"

"Yeah," she said, "but 99 percent of the time, it's *you* who does that!"

And so began a funny argument in the Daly household. Jean, by giving Trent some money, remembered not something I actually *did*, but something she *thinks* I do, and far too often — give the kids money. I had nothing to do with what happened at the Dollar Store, but in her mind, I stood guilty. For her, loaning out six bucks seemed less an issue involving her and Trent but more an extension of an ongoing parenting problem of *mine*!

Do I give the kids money too often? I don't think so, because I don't really carry cash — but then again, that's *my* perception of reality, isn't it?

This sort of thing happens in families all the time. Sometimes these disagreements become fodder for ongoing family jokes, and other times these different perspectives — these different perceptions of reality—can cause real problems. How many husbands and wives argue about who does more around the house? About who spends money less wisely? About who takes a greater role in disciplining the kids? These very serious issues tend to grow more serious with time. Sometimes these arguments illuminate real problems, because lots of dads out there really don't chip in nearly enough around the house or spend enough time with the kids. And yes, I am guilty of *that*. Lots of moms might be guilty of a number of household sins themselves. But most often, it comes down to a matter of perspective, and the arguments don't do anything to uncover the truth. Instead they just throw more dirt on top of it.

Couples need to find a way to get on the same page, to come to a consensus on where the weaknesses really lie. The earlier you can do that, the more effectively you can learn from it and work together in uncovering reality. The more effectively you and your partner can understand where reality lies, the better you can teach your children about that reality.

Is this easy? No way. Jean and I are still working on it. Most couples never cross the finish line in gauging reality. It's always a work in progress.

Different Strokes for Different ... Parents

It all gets complicated by the fact that every mom and every dad differs from every other mom and dad. We think differently. We act differently. We even teach differently. We can explain some of those differences by our respective genders. But it goes beyond that and into our differences as individuals —the unique characteristics, attributes, and outlooks that God has given each of us.

Consider the issue of regular devotions, another point of friction in the Daly household.

Now, Jean and I agree that we need to give Trent and Troy an understanding of and appreciation and respect for God and his Word. That's our number one job. And Jean is incredibly thoughtful and proactive in teaching those things. Every night, almost without fail, she makes sure we have an evening devotional time after dinner. We read the Bible, talk about Scripture, and pray. That's all great — except that sometimes the kids can get a little squirmy. (Frankly, I can too.) So Jean feels the burden of our devotions more than I do. And she can get frustrated at times because I don't take on a larger role during that time, that I don't always seem to back her up the way she feels I should. Sometimes she can feel as though I don't take the kids' spiritual training as seriously as I ought to. She sees herself carrying more of that load.

But for me, life's teachable moments — those times when real training happens — are almost always fluid. They come in the moment, when a topic comes up or the time feels right. And a lot of times, those moments take place in the car or as we're out walking or engaged in some other activity. I might talk with the boys about what their day was like — whether they saw it as a great or a not-so-great day. We use those issues as springboards to talk about other stuff. I pray with them every time I take them to school. Jean isn't there to see that, of course, so even though she knows it's happening, it doesn't necessarily help when she feels stressed and unappreciated during our evening devotions. Nor does she think that what I do in the car takes the place — or *should* take the place — of the purposeful time we spend together as a family.

Jean is a teacher at heart. She likes the structure of devotions. She likes sitting down and talking through issues and celebrating God purposefully and intentionally. I'm a very spontaneous guy. I love to do things in the moment. I believe I'm getting the job done as a dad, even though I do so while in motion.

In these moments, we don't struggle with a different reality. We both see the end goal clearly. But we want to take different pathways to get to that ultimate truth, and sometimes we doubt that a way other than our own might lead just as effectively to the same point. Instead of arguing about whether the sculpture is green or yellow, we argue about whether it's greenish-yellow or yellowish-green, all the while believing that it really and truly matters.

The challenge Jean and I now face is how to embrace these different ways of teaching without denigrating one or the other. How can I better help her see that I'm not shirking my spiritual responsibilities? And just as importantly, how can I show the boys how worthwhile and meaningful those evening devotions can be? How can I better support Jean?

This issue isn't unique to Jean and me. Almost every couple with kids has moments when they feel this tension. Maybe it's not about a family devotional time, but it's about homework or getting chores done. Whatever it is, these moments provide challenges. And each couple works through them differently.

But that being said, we dads have two key points to keep in mind as we work through these issues. First, we must support our wives in whatever they try to do for our kids. We have to back them up without fail. We must always be asking how we can better come alongside and help them. And second, while it's critical to support moms, it's just as important to lead your kids in a way that feels comfortable to *you*. And for me, that means teaching them in the midst of doing something.

Boys Will Be Boys

The differences Jean and I have in teaching and raising our boys are specific to us as individuals, to who we are and how God has wired us. But some of our tension points can illustrate general differences between the way men and women operate, particularly when it comes to their kids.

Jean's level of comfort with formal devotions speaks to her scientific, orderly bent. But it also speaks to her femininity. Women tend to feel much more comfortable sitting at the kitchen table and talking through issues than men do. Moms usually like to go deep. And to do that, they feel that they, and their kids, must remain still.

But most guys probably don't operate like that. When I talk, I do so in motion, which is very much a guy thing. I want to do activity in the midst of my teaching. Let me shoot some hoops. Let me play with Legos. Let me do anything but sit still. And even when we're not talking, the activities themselves can teach valuable lessons. Anyone who's ever taken a driver to a golf ball knows the game itself can teach the importance of patience and perseverance (and not breaking a club over one's knee).

We dads shouldn't try to mother our kids. Moms already do a great job of that. They nurture, care for, and talk with their sons and daughters in a way we could never hope to duplicate. Instead, we dads need to be *fathers* to our children. We must interact with them in ways that only fathers can. And one element of that, very often, is teaching lessons, not on a sofa over tea, but through action.

Years ago, I'd take the boys to Home Depot or Lowe's for their Saturday hobby days — days when kids would learn how to build a birdhouse or a fire truck out of little kits the stores provided. Those mornings became great times for fellowship with Trent and Troy, and in a way, they offered a little spiritual training as well. Think about a five-year-old trying to drive a nail into a piece of balsa wood — it requires a lot of patience. Or how building a birdhouse can focus a child's attention and encourage him or her to follow through with even difficult tasks. Those projects taught my boys something about frustration, perseverance, and the reward of a job well done. But some moms wouldn't see those lessons: They'd think that Dad just took the boys out for a morning to have a little fun. But a lot is happening in the midst of all that fun. Trent and Troy didn't just build little wooden racers on those hobby mornings; they built character.

I'm a firm believer in teaching through action. The most important life lessons I ever learned as a kid or teen came while I was doing something, whether it was out on the playground or the practice field or participating in a Fellowship of Christian Athletes conference with my buddies. Men are, on the whole, persons of action. We learn best when we're not *trying* to learn at all. We need an activity to distract us so the lessons can sink in.

Even now, I'm talking with my boys about getting them golf lessons so they can golf with me. We're talking about learning how to fly-fish so we can go fishing together. Already I have in mind a picture from the book *A River Runs Through It* — two boys and their dad, fishing on a river in Montana, talking about their lives and their experiences and God. We can learn a lot of lessons while standing in the middle of a river. I'm sure of it.

Minding the Moment

It gets back to what I talked about at the beginning of the book — finding those moments with your children. Those moments provide special, unforgettable opportunities. Those moments are critically important for a host of reasons, some of which I'll describe in the next chapter. But one of the biggest is that when they are taught some lesson in that moment, they never forget it. The message and the moment become inseparable. "I remember when my dad and I went rock climbing and we talked about perseverance," your boy might say. Or "I remember when my dad and I went out to get my ears pierced and he talked to me about purity."

And here's the thing: While the moments become special through the lessons we share, the moments themselves don't have to be all that remarkable. You don't have to do a tandem skydive with your son or daughter if you want to communicate a point. Sometimes you can just throw around a baseball or share a soda at the mall. Even a simple drive can help loosen tongues and get an important conversation rolling. The message and the moment work together to make a memory.

Recently, Troy and I went up into the mountains for a special father-son retreat. On the way up, we had The Talk. You know, *The* Talk. For me, The Talk is actually three separate discussions in which the stuff gets lumped into different buckets. In the first discussion, I talk about how God designed us in his image, both male and female, and then explain what that means. The second discusses the biblical institution of marriage and what *that* means. And in the third, we get into the physical mechanics of it all.

So as I went over the third bucket with him — getting into some potentially embarrassing subject matter on our way to the mountains — he took it all in stride. The road was rolling under the wheels, and I talked about wet dreams and intercourse and all sorts of stuff. He just took it all in.

"Are you with me?" I asked every once in a while.

"Uh-huh," he'd say.

"Well, if you have any questions, just go ahead and ask," I said. "Just ask whatever's in your mind, and I'll try to answer."

We had driven another ten or fifteen minutes down the road when suddenly Troy turned to me and said, "Dad, I have a question. Do I have to remember that 'm' word?"

I thought for a second. "What, you mean *masturbation*? No, no. You don't have to worry about the word. I'll talk to you more about it when you get older."

"Oh," Troy said, "that's good. I was a little worried. That's a big word to remember."

I'm guessing Troy will recall that conversation on the road to the mountains for the rest of his life. I know I will.

Lessons in Love

No matter how you like to teach, whether formally, informally, or in some other way, one critical element must be a part of your lesson — love.

"Love is patient, love is kind," Paul wrote in 1 Corinthians 13:4 – 5. "It does not envy, it does not boast, it is not proud. It does not dishonor others, it is not self-seeking, it is not easily angered, it keeps no record of wrongs." These bedrock principles tell us not just how to care for one another but also how to teach our children effectively. Whether we're leading devotions or having The Talk or even finding ourselves in the middle of a necessary, stern rebuke, we must always stay mindful of how much we love our kids. We must be patient with them and kind. We shouldn't bring up past wrongdoings without reason. We should always show them respect. These are good principles to remember not just for the sake of our children but also for the sake of the *lesson*. Truth is, when we "teach" out of anger or frustration, when we scold or belittle or turn red with rage, the lessons rarely stick. Our kids forget the lessons and remember the anger. They forget the point and remember the pain.

Although none of the "fathers" in my life tried to teach me much, my real dad showed me what a good lesson can look like.

I was probably about five years old when a neighbor girl and I started playing doctor with each other. There was nothing sexual about it at all; as curious children, we felt amazed we each had different parts.

My sister, Dee Dee, caught us, and I imagine she was thrilled with the prospect of getting little Jimmy in trouble. She grabbed me by the arm, marched me all the way back to the house, and pushed me right in front of Dad.

"I caught Jimmy playing doctor with a girl down the street!" she said. I'm sure she looked confident in her arrest and conviction, but I didn't notice. I felt too embarrassed and scared to care.

My dad looked at both of us. "I see," he said. "Dee Dee, can you leave us be for a moment?"

Dee Dee gave me a wicked, "you're gonna get it" smile as she wheeled around and left the room, very proud of herself. But as soon as she had gone, my dad smiled at me.

"The differences between boys and girls," he said with a little chuckle, "that's a good thing. But it's not an appropriate thing for you to show yourself to girls, or for girls to show themselves to you. Don't do it again, all right?"

And that was it. He handed out no punishment and refused to get heavy-handed. He used a little light humor. He didn't go crazy. Right then, my dad rose above the moment. He remained mindful of who I was. He understood a child's curiosity. He knew that people, particularly little kids, make mistakes. We're all fallible. And I wonder now if his own failings made him more aware and sympathetic to those of other people. Maybe the fact that he was so aware of his own shortcomings helped him better understand and accept the shortcomings of others. Maybe he knew that mistakes are a part of life. Failure finds a place in everyone's background. He knew that, and he accepted that. And it gave him the ability to be kind and patient in that moment — a rare good memory I have of my dad.

Isn't that how our heavenly Father understands us? He remembers we are dust — frail and fallible human beings. God, even in his perfection, has a much better understanding of our own imperfections than we do. It's not a matter of *if* we mess up, but *when* and *how badly*. He knows it will happen, and he forgives us when it does. God just wants us to learn from it.

I'm trying my best to become a good teacher, a kind and patient teacher, to my kids. I think about my own dad and how gentle he could be. I think about my eternal Father and how kind and forgiving he is. And now that my kids are getting older, I stay mindful of my own mistakes and imperfections, teaching through those very mistakes if it seems appropriate and meaningful. Even pieces of my own story can become teachable moments. Maybe by talking about some of my own missteps, I can help my children avoid them.

I've always wanted to be pretty open with my boys. I don't tell them about all the mistakes I made, but when it seems appropriate and my experience tells me something might help them, I do. And as they get older, I'll get even more open. The older they get, the more they can handle.

Trent and Troy are thirteen and eleven now, and I think they've reached that next stage of learning, that next stage of growth. And I believe, very strongly, that I'm coming into my time as a teacher.

In years gone by, Jean took the lead in the teaching department. She'd nurture them and take care of them and coach them in most of the ways they needed. I helped reinforce those lessons and taught a few of my own, but Jean really drove the show. I believe that many families operate in a similar way. Mothers, after all, are the constant in the family. More often than not, they ensure that their children have the best foundation. If they were the ones in charge of sending our kids off to sea, they'd build the boats. They'd make the hull sound and watertight. They'd make the boat hard to capsize and as safe and seaworthy as possible.

But as kids grow up, dads take on a bigger role. And I feel that responsibility keenly now. I'm the one who has to come alongside Trent and Troy and tell them what it means to be a man. What it means to be an adult. What it means to make your own decisions and find your own way, yet still always follow God.

If Mom makes the boat, then Dad hoists the sail. We help our kids catch the wind, teach them how to use it, and, when they're ready, help them glide away.

This process has already begun in our home. When Trent was about to turn thirteen, I sat down with him for a chat.

"I'm going to start talking to you more like an adult now," I told him. "It's going to be more man-to-man, not man-to-boy." When I said it, his whole face lit up. He *wants* to be a man, as all boys do. That, after all, is what all our teaching, training, and coaching is designed to help him become — a man.

All boys want to become men. All girls want to become women. God made us that way, having instilled in us a desire to grow up and make decisions and teach lessons of our own. As Trent and Troy grow, we'll look for markers on the way to manhood, moments that show their journey toward a new age of growth and responsibility. Jean and I will teach them everything we can along the way. We'll show them reality as best we can so that as they begin making more of their own decisions, they'll make them with a clear eye and uncluttered mind. And when they make mistakes, as they will, we'll do our best to come alongside in kindness and love and help them recalibrate their steps to get to where they need to go.

And then when they are ready to set sail on their own, we'll be there to see them off, watching as they glide toward the sunrise.

——— TO THINK ABOUT ———

1. What's the most important lesson your father taught you? How did he teach it?

2. Do you think you and your wife have a good handle on reality? Do your sense of reality and hers sometimes differ? What sort of friction does that cause? How can you get those realities to better align?

3. What three things would you like to teach your children before they leave home? Are you teaching those lessons now? How? Do you think those lessons are sinking in?

Nine

Getting Messy

Troy and I just got back from an adventure, the same adventure we were on when we had The Talk.

It's called Colorado Adventure, fittingly enough, a camp outside Yampa, Colorado, specially designed for kids twelve and under and their dads. We rode horses, shot a few arrows, and even did a little ranch work — cutting cattle (separating steers from cows while on horseback). And naturally, since it's a Christian camp (sponsored by Focus on the Family), we did an awful lot of talking and praying and fellowshipping. The whole experience is about investing in your child, and in that sort of natural environment, kids tend to get really honest with their fathers. Dads and kids go off into the woods for an hour at a time and just talk. Our kids have a chance to tell us what we do that makes them feel good and not-so-good. We dads tell our kids how much we love and appreciate them, and why. The last night, we do a blessing where each father stands with his son or daughter by the campfire and blesses them. We had some tremendous conversations, and Troy and I had a blast.

That is, we did until Saturday night, the last night at camp, when I blessed my son and told him how much he meant to me.

"Dad," Troy said when we got back to the tent, looking a little green, "I'm not feeling very good."

Uh-oh, I thought. We're in a tent in the middle of the forest, with no toilet anywhere close and the nearest bottle of Pepto-Bismol many miles away.

But hey, he'll probably do just fine. And if not, we're roughing it, right? Just one more authentic experience to put in the journal. It's not like the cowboys or fur trappers of yesteryear didn't get the occasional sour stomach. So I did what any good cowboy or trapper surely would've done. I put a big sack — one of those covers that you stuff sleeping bags into — beside Troy.

"Okay, so Troy," I said, "if you feel like you're going to get sick, here's a big bag. Right there beside you. If you have to get sick, just barf in the bag and we'll toss it out afterward."

"Okay," he said. And then we turned in for the night. I hoped that Troy wouldn't get sick, but if he did, we'd be covered.

Around 2:00 a.m., I woke up to one of the worst noises a father can hear in a tent — BLWWAAAP!

The sound of Troy throwing up. It was pitch-black, and the only sound anywhere was my son repeatedly retching. Even the crickets stopped to listen. I fumbled for my headlamp, but I couldn't find it.

"Troy?" I asked, feeling frantically for the light (and a little worried I might put my hand in something disgusting). "You all right?"

"BLWWAAAP!" Troy repeated.

Finally, I found the light, flipped it on, and saw that Troy had indeed thrown up — but not in the sack. It looked, for a moment, like it had gone everywhere. I'd given the child just one little task ...

"Oh, Troy," I said. And I must've sounded more annoyed than concerned.

"I'm sorry, Dad," Troy said, a little feebly. "I couldn't help it. I'm sorry."

"Okay, okay," I sighed. "Let's just get you cleaned up."

After further examining the mess, I saw that Troy had, purely by accident, thrown up on what might have been the next best thing to a bag — a foam mat. He must've retched three or four times, and none of it got onto the tent itself. So at least that was *something* we could be thankful for.

But of all the things we had done at the camp to this point, none of them taught me anything about how to deal with a vomiting boy in a tent. That's probably why I sounded so irritated to Troy; I had no idea what to do. And if dads hate anything, it's to be clueless in moments of crisis.

We shoved the mat and all of Troy's messed-up clothes into the farthest corner of the tent. Troy, naturally, felt a lot better. In seconds he'd fallen back asleep. Meanwhile, I spent the rest of the night with my face pressed up to one of the vents in the tent, frantically trying to inhale some fresh, untainted air. "Please, God," I prayed silently, "give me oxygen."

But during that long, long night, I had some time to reflect on the irony of it all. Just hours before, Troy and I had walked in the forest. I'd had my arm around his shoulder and told him how much I loved him and that I'd always love him, no matter what. And now, I felt annoyed and irritated because Troy hadn't thrown up where I wanted him to.

Stress can do that to us, whether intense or mild. When we hit a bump in the road, all our unconditional love and good intentions can disappear, leaving us holding a bag full of anger, disappointment, and exasperation. Troy didn't know what to do that night, and I didn't know what to do — and that's probably why I felt so irritated. In the end, I couldn't do much. I couldn't get up and clean it up, since we had no running water, no towels to wipe up the mess, nothing. Realistically, we could do only one thing — wait till morning.

That night reminded me of one of my weaknesses. I tend to respond pretty well when something really bad happens. If fire or flood or fender bender should come, I'm your man. But I have far less confidence in my ability to deal with the bad grade or the dirty room or the vomit in the tent. It's the little things that sometimes drag me down. It's the little things I have to watch out for.

I don't think either of us learned a lot of practical, takeaway lessons that night. Maybe next trip I'll bring a couple of garbage bags, just in case. But the incident did serve as a reminder of what I as a dad could work on. I need to watch my tone of voice when I get stressed. I have to do my best to stay calm. And when I tell my kids that I love them unconditionally, I must work hard to show them my love in what I say and how I say it, in what I do and how I do it — even when the vomit hits the fan.

It's funny how God uses adversity in our lives, isn't it? Truth is, I think he works best when we have a bit of mess to clean up. He teaches us most effectively when we feel a little stressed.

We may like the comfort of tranquility, but I wonder if it's overrated.

Express in the Mess

I like a little ruckus in the family. I like life to get a little messy. God can work through that mess and in the end do some pretty amazing things.

Some of this conviction comes right out of my own experiences. My whole childhood was one big mess from the time I hit age five, and yet that mess helped make me the man I am today.

Now, don't take that to mean your kids will excel in life if you make them suffer. Don't say to yourself, "Well, forget this fatherhood thing. Daly says he was better off without a father."

That's not true at all. I wouldn't wish my childhood on anybody. The primary reason I'm writing this book is to illustrate the critical importance of fathers, and I want to encourage you to become the kind of father I never had. Your kids deserve a good dad. They *need* a good dad. Statistically, few things are more important to a child's development than a strong, loving father. God designed it that way.

But God also designed us to need a little stress in our lives. A little pain. It sounds strange, I know. We don't like to think of God working through our pain. But he does it all the time. And he can do it in really unexpected ways.

The Best Break Ever

As a seventeen-year-old, I earned the job of starting senior quarterback for Yucca Valley High School. And frankly, I was pretty good.

I had a killer right arm and a can-do attitude. In the huddle, people looked to me for leadership. They felt confident I could get the job done, no matter the deficit — and if they lacked confidence, it didn't matter. I had confidence to spare. College scouts sent me letters of interest, and I knew it was just a matter of time before a big-time program called and asked for a commitment. And if I played for a big-name school, who knows? Could the pros be in the offing too? I didn't see why not.

I also lacked adult supervision. My mom had died. My myriad father figures had left the picture. I lived with my brother, Dave, which meant I could pretty much go anywhere and do anything I liked. My friends and I hung out all weekend after the games. Girls smiled kindly at me. Sure, I'd been a Christian for a couple of years, but I didn't have any real desire to act like one, at least not on the weekends when a pretty girl showed some interest in me. What did Augustine say? "Give me chastity and continence, but not yet."

Then Mike, my older brother who played college football, told me I was getting a big head about myself. "You gotta mellow out," he told me. "You're not all that."

Except I am all that, part of me thought. *And after all, I'm a quarterback. Quarterbacks need a little ego.*

But another part of me, the Christian part, the Spirit within me, wondered whether Mike was right. Part of me wondered whether as fun as being a hot-shot high school quarterback was, it might not have been real healthy, spiritually speaking.

And so on a Saturday afternoon, right before a game against Big Bear High School, I knelt down and offered one of the strangest prayers I've ever said: *Lord, if you don't want me to play big-time college football because it'll take me in the wrong direction, then break a bone today. But don't let it hurt.*

So the game began. Sometime during the first half, one of our players got punched in the pile, and he stood up and took a swing at the guy. Of course, our player, one of our best blockers, got ejected from the game. Now, in four years of high school ball, I'd never seen that happen. After our coach made a couple of player adjustments, a sophomore came into the huddle to play fullback, his eyes as big as saucers.

"What should I do?" he asked me. Not the sort of question that inspires a lot of confidence.

But remember, I had confidence to spare. "Step to my right," I told him, "and hit somebody inside-out." Simple, right?

I took the snap and dropped back, ready to pass. Out of the corner of my eye, I saw a linebacker, a huge, fast guy, breaking through the line. Our fullback stood there and then suddenly jumped *out* of the guy's way. I kid you not. It was like he dove away from a speeding semi. Which, in a way, I guess he did.

As I released the throw, the next thing I knew, the linebacker hit me smack underneath the armpit. I hit the turf, nothing that hadn't happened about a thousand times before. But when I tried to push myself up, I felt a strange pressure around my shoulder pads. I walked slowly back to the huddle and reached under my shoulder pads to my left collarbone, where I felt a sharp protrusion underneath the skin. I didn't feel any real pain unless I lifted up my arm too far, but I knew what had happened. The guy had snapped my collarbone almost in two.

"Guys," I said in the huddle, "I think God answered my prayer."

No Pain, No Gain

I don't know the theology of broken bones, but I know that God was with me that afternoon. No one will ever be able to convince me otherwise. That broken collarbone ended my football career, but it steered me in a new direction — a better direction. God brought me back to him and led me to where I am today. God worked through my sins and my pride. He worked through my prayer. And he worked through a broken bone.

Don't let it hurt, I had prayed. And I think most of us make that same plea to God every day of our lives, whether or not we say the words. *Don't let it hurt. Don't let* me *hurt.* We want to lead pain-free lives. We don't want to deal with stress or pressure. We want to escape all that.

And yet, somehow, the Lord uses pain and stress to teach us.

Think about what happens when you lift weights. Every time you do a biceps curl or bench press, the pressure creates tiny tears in your muscle tissue. After a day or so, those tears heal themselves, making the muscle a bit bigger, a bit stronger.

Or think about how we build up our hearts and lungs. To keep them healthy, we walk, run, or use a rowing machine, all to put reasonable stress on our bodies and keep them working as they should. We need to put a little tension on our bodies to keep them healthy.

We run our brains through their paces too. Tests and quizzes can sharpen the mind. Word and math computer programs can keep mental faculties limber. A game of chess can strain the brain, but the more we play chess, the better we get at it and the sharper our minds grow. Scientists now say that for those who want their minds to stay quick and stave off memory loss as they grow older, it's a good idea to give your brain a good workout every day.

If God made our bodies and minds to grow under stress, then why should our spirits be any different?

The apostle Paul tells us in Romans that we should "glory in our sufferings." Why? "Because we know that suffering produces perseverance; perseverance, character; and character, hope. And hope does not put us to shame, because God's love has been poured out into our hearts through the Holy Spirit, who has been given to us" (Romans 5:3 – 5).

That doesn't mean we should look for ways to inflict severe pain on our kids. No good dad wants to inflict too much stress or suffering on his son or daughter. That goes against our nature. But we shouldn't try to protect them as much as we might like to. We shouldn't try to save them from every little stress and pain they might experience. After all, pressure and pain are an inevitable part of life, and we're supposed to be teaching our kids how to deal with life in all of its sometimes messy and painful wonder.

In fact, parents use well-placed pain to teach. They have to. It's one of the most effective ways to curb unsafe or unwise behavior, and it really follows the path set down by God in nature. If we hold our hand over the flame, the pain tells us we shouldn't do such a thing again. If we get sick from eating a few mysterious berries growing outside our caves, we learn to stay away from those berries. When we read the Bible, we see plenty of instances where God punishes his people, not because he's mean, but because he wants to teach them the right way to behave so as to glorify him.

In the same way, parents must lay out fair but unmistakable consequences for when their kids go astray. If they lie to us, for instance, or fail to clean their rooms like we asked them to, or if they're mistreating their little brothers, we punish them. Sometimes we might take away some of their favorite toys or ground them for a week. Sometimes we might administer a swift swat on the rear. But whatever we choose to do, any punishment we dole out is a form of pain. We hope our kids will try to avoid that pain and do what they ought to do, the next time around. We don't punish to be mean or because we feel angry or vengeful. We punish because we love our kids. We want what's best for them, and we know that a little pain now can ward off a whole lot more down the road. It's all part of being a good dad.

I think our twenty-first-century, safety-conscious culture sometimes keeps us dads from allowing our kids to take a few risks. We have an insatiable appetite for safety. We minimize risk as much as we can. We try to eliminate every conceivable danger. If we see a kid riding in the back of a pickup truck, we assume the driver is just asking to get pulled over for child abuse. Children risk being expelled from school if they make a "gun" out of a Pop-Tart.

Hey, I want our kids safe too. I'm all for that. But I think this preoccupation — obsession, really — with safety harms our kids.

I can remember the days when we'd let a child struggle to climb a tree instead of putting him on a limb where he wanted to perch. A lot of parents rush to the aid of their son or daughter the moment they start to climb the maple tree out front. We don't like to see our kids fail. And so, more often than not, we pick up the kids and put them in the tree — staying close enough to catch them should they lose their balance and fall.

This could get me in trouble, but I think a dad isn't necessarily his best when he helps his child sit in a tree. He's at his best when he lets them climb it on their own.

At first, they'll probably fail. And fail again. They might even fall. But you know what? Cuts and scrapes heal. Bruises fade. Even broken bones knit back together. Maybe that sounds harsh, but I doubt you should wrap up your kids in bubble wrap for their childhood. It's neither good nor healthy for them. Let a kid *live*. Let him climb the tree. Let him struggle and even suffer a little. Let him fail so he can try again the next time. We learn so much from our mistakes, so give your kids a chance to make some.

Suffering breeds perseverance, Paul tells us. And perseverance, character. And character, hope. How will children ever develop perseverance if their parents always put them in the tree? Where's the persevering in that? No character gets developed. Instead it's all about "I get what I want."

We so strongly want to protect our kids. We want to keep them from harm — and not just physical harm, but emotional as well. We give them all sorts of safety nets and "attaboys." We tell them they're awesome before they've even done anything — gold stars just for trying. And yet, our culture seems ever more despondent, ever more discouraged. According to the advocacy organization Mental Health America, one in five teens may suffer from depression, and those numbers are increasing "at an alarming rate."[29] About 4,600 youth between the ages of ten and twenty-four commit suicide every year, making it the third leading cause of death among that age group.[30] In 2011, Gallup asked Americans whether today's teens would be better off than their parents. Only 44 percent said yes, an all-time low.[31]

I know many factors come into play when we talk about depression and suicide — mental illness, bullying, any number of societal ills. But when I look at those stats, I wonder whether our coddling culture plays a part too. If we don't allow our children to take risks, even if those risks entail a little suffering, how are we helping them learn perseverance? And if they don't persevere, how can they grow their character? And if their character isn't growing, where does hope come from? From parents who put their kids in the tree? From peewee football games where they don't keep score? Hope doesn't come from those places. Those places generate a sense of entitlement, maybe. An unrealistic expectation that *someone* will keep them from all harm, perhaps. But hope? I don't think so.

We have to fight the instinct to solve every problem for them. We have to stifle our urge to become a magical cure-all for our kids and be, instead, a dad.

We have to let our kids take risks. Sure, risks can lead to mistakes. They can even lead to failure. But in those mistakes, even in the failings, our children's character is unpacked. In those dark times of stress and suffering they learn. And out of those lessons they develop real confidence, not the artificial kind that comes when their fathers stick them up in a tree, but the real kind, the kind that lets them know they can climb that blasted maple because they've done it. It didn't happen right away, and they have the skinned knees to prove it. But in the end, they got it done. They conquered that tree. And if they can climb that tree, who knows what else they can do?

Being There

But just because we stand aside for a bit and let our children risk failure, it doesn't mean we dads stay uninvolved. In fact, in times like these, in the midst of these risk-taking opportunities, we must remain more present than ever.

A couple of weeks before Troy and I had our unforgettable adventure, Trent and I went on a different father-child retreat — Adventures in Fatherhood, a Focus program held every year near Yosemite National Park. The four-day event is a real back-to-basics excursion. There are no cabins, no bathrooms, not even any tents. When you sleep, you sleep under the stars — just your sleeping bag and a thin mat separating you from the granite beneath. When you go to the bathroom, you have to pack it in the "dunny" bucket and take it out with you (yes, paper and all). For folks who think that roughing it means going without Wi-Fi service, Adventures in Fatherhood provides a rude, but often welcome, awakening.

And that's the point. Every moment of the excursion is designed to push dads and their kids a little out of their comfort zone — to challenge them in new ways and, through those challenges, to help fathers and their sons and daughters get closer.

And the obstacles get *way* bigger than packing out your own poop.

The biggest obstacle? I think of the Prowl, a 180-foot granite cliff that towers over the forest floor like a ship piercing the ocean. Keep in mind that 180 feet corresponds to the height of a fifteen-story building. Looking over the edge can make almost anyone dizzy. And we had to rappel down that thing. Fathers and children alike are invited to hop over the edge, in tandem, and slide down two perfectly safe (but frighteningly thin) ropes until they hit bottom — one way or another.

Not everyone looks forward to the Prowl. In fact, I think most kids, and most parents too, have a little trepidation when their turn comes. Before you begin the rappel, one guide asks the kids, on a scale of one to ten, how confident they feel. Are they scared? Excited? Both?

"I'm about a three," one boy said. "I'm pretty nervous."

A girl reported she was about a seven. She knew everything would be fine, but it still looked a long way down.

And then came Trent's turn to speak.

"Ten," he said, without hesitation.

"Really?" the guide asked. "We don't get a lot of tens here."

"I just wanna go down," Trent answered, grinning as wide as I'd ever seen him.

And down we went. True to his word, he never showed any sign of fear or nervousness. Not when guides strapped him into his harness and not when he put in place the carabiner (a metal device used to slow or break our progress down the rope). Not when we hopped over the edge. Not halfway down, when I realized that my excess weight wouldn't allow me to keep the steady pace of my son. Some twenty years and fifty pounds earlier, I'd done the Prowl. And now those extra fifty pounds tugged me down the rope.

"Trent, I'd love to hang out with you," I said, as I zipped farther ahead, "but man, I gotta go."

When we both reached the bottom, I think Trent felt pretty impressed with the speed with which his old man rappelled down the Prowl. He must've thought, temporarily at least, *He's more of a daredevil than I'd imagined.*

"Dad, you were going so fast!"

"I had to," I admitted.

Developing Character, Growing Confidence

Over the course of those four days, I watched Trent blossom. The environment out there, as rough and raw as it is, fit him perfectly. The caution he typically displays had vanished. His gangly, thirteen-year-old body — the same body that he worries looks awkward and uncoordinated — was (and is) perfect for rock climbing. His spindly arms and legs could reach obscure handholds and footholds. The same lanky strength that sometimes was a liability in team sports found a new expression on those California rock faces. He was good, and he could feel it. You could see the confidence fill him. And that preteen irritability he'd been showing in the last year or so simply disappeared in that environment.

He didn't feel *comfortable* in that environment. In fact, exactly the opposite. He was being challenged, not just physically, but emotionally and socially. Other than me, he didn't know the people with us. He didn't necessarily feel at ease sharing his heart in front of a bunch of strangers, as we all had to do during the four days. He wasn't used to any of this stuff.

He found himself totally out of his element. And yet Trent felt completely at home.

We find ourselves in the midst of risk. In the mess and the dust of life, we grow to understand who we are, who we can be, and, most importantly, who God wants us to be. No one can simply confer confidence to a person. They have to earn it.

At night, Trent and I returned to our sleeping area, separated from other campers, and we'd look at the stars. We'd bundle up in our beanies and our long underwear and talk about the vastness of God. We'd marvel at his incredible creation, and then we'd remind ourselves that we human beings, as insignificant as we feel sometimes, are the pinnacle, the crown jewel, of that creation. Of all the things that lie in front of us — the trees, the mountains, the mighty Prowl — God values us above them all.

We sometimes find it hard to appreciate how special we are in God's eyes. I think it can be especially hard for a twelve-year-old whose body is changing in uncomfortable ways, whose powerful emotions can be confusing, and who can sometimes feel very unlovable — a walking, talking mess. *How could anyone care for me?*

As a father, it can feel frustrating to try to lead your child through that time. Sometimes nothing you say will make much difference. They'll still get frustrated with themselves. They'll get angry. They'll feel at times a little worthless.

But the moments arise when you can come alongside your son or daughter and help show them how special they are. You can watch them strive. You can encourage them. But in the end, they have to discover the truth on their own. They have to climb their own tree. And when they succeed, when they show that perseverance, character, and hope, you'll know the work was worth it.

Make the Most of the Mess

We've talked a lot about moments in this book, the stories that shape us and define us, whether father or mother, son or daughter. I see those moments as critical. And very often, those moments involve mess. They involve risk. Almost by definition, they occur when something out of the ordinary happens, something unexpected that forces us to adjust our expectations and even ourselves. We don't create a lot of moments by sitting on our butts and watching football all weekend. (And yes, I'm guilty of that too.)

Think of those moments we try to create as something like the monuments and memorials created by Abraham and Jacob and the nation of Israel when it first came into being.

When something remarkable happened, they'd often build something — a well, an altar, a monument — to commemorate it. In the book of Joshua, for instance, we hear how the Lord miraculously dammed the Jordan River, allowing his chosen people to cross the swollen waters. After they crossed, the Bible tells us that "Joshua set up the twelve stones that had been in the middle of the Jordan at the spot where the priests who carried the ark of the covenant had stood" (Joshua 4:9). It was, literally, a rock-solid reminder of the great thing God had done in their lives. The people built these monuments so that those who came after them would never forget it.

The moments we make function something like that. They serve as monuments in our children's hearts to remind them what that moment meant. For Trent, the Prowl may be one of those monumental moments. Every time he remembers rappelling down that rock face, he'll remember the confidence it took to do it. He'll remember how good it felt to have that confidence. And I hope this memory will apply to other aspects of his life. *I was good enough then*, he might think. *I'm good enough now to face this new challenge. I did that; I can do this.*

And should for some reason Trent forget, I'll be there to remind him. I'll leverage that moment when he feels low. When he's playing football for the first time and misses a block or something, I'll have a chance to say, "Do you remember the Prowl? Remember that confidence you felt? Think about that the next time you run that play."

But you don't need to rappel off a 180-foot cliff to create a moment. Sometimes the real risk is getting off the couch and doing *something*—anything at all. Want to make a mess? Make it in the kitchen and help your kids whip up a batch of cookies, particularly if neither you nor they have ever made cookies. Want to take a chance? Visit the local putt-putt course and chance smacking your ball into a stupid windmill five or six times. Want to get risky? Put your pride on the line by playing a video game with your sons.

There isn't much that can humble me more than playing Super Mario Bros. with my boys. In this cooperative game, we all push to complete the same tasks. And in this virtual world, I'm definitely the weak link.

"Come on, Dad," they'll implore. "Jump higher!" I always lag behind in that game, which makes it exactly the opposite of where we are in reality, when I'm trying to pull them along in life. But the role reversal is good for all of us. We laugh a lot about it. In their own small way, those embarrassing Mario Bros. sessions make for moments of their own. "Remember how horrible Dad was at video games?" I can hear Trent remind Troy at a Thanksgiving dinner twenty years from now. We'll all laugh again—and I'll be feeling grateful that we packed up the Wii fifteen years earlier.

Finding moments for you and your children to share

doesn't have to take a lot of expense. It doesn't even necessarily take a lot of time. But it's critical to find a moment in *something*. Put your kids in a not-so-safe environment where God can push them a little. Don't put them in danger, obviously, but let them feel a little risk. Give them a chance to take a chance. If they succeed, great. If they fail, that's great too — because either way, they learn something.

That's the beauty of these moments, the beauty of the mess. We find ourselves there. Sometimes we get a better understanding of who God wants us to be. So let them risk their talent. Let them stretch. Let them see what God will show them.

──────────── **TO THINK ABOUT** ────────────

1. When have you learned something about yourself in the middle of a mess?

2. Do you like to take risks? Describe the last risk you took.

3. Is it hard for you to let your children take risks of their own? Do you encourage them to take chances? Have you ever seen your child learn something in a messy or risky moment?

4. Do you ever take risks of your own with your children? Risks that could embarrass you?

Ten

Before It's Too Late

I ONCE HEARD A STORY ABOUT A GIRL WHO HATED HER father.

I don't know why she hated him. I don't know for how long. But I get the sense that the disconnect was mutual. For ages, the two never spoke to one another, never set eyes on each other. But as the years rolled by, the girl, now a woman, began to regret the split. She wanted to reconnect with her dad, but she didn't know how. She made a couple of calls home, which never got returned. And eventually she just gave up.

Shortly before Father's Day, she realized that her dad would be nearly eighty now. Perhaps he didn't have many Father's Days left. Whatever had caused the breach in their relationship happened decades before — practically forgotten now. The woman was a different person. And so, she hoped, was her father.

And so she bought him a Father's Day card. She meant to write out just a short note and perhaps a phone number, inviting him to call her. But she found she couldn't. Instead, she wrote a long, heartfelt letter and placed it inside the card. She expressed regrets. She offered apologies. She told her dad how much she missed him, how much she *had* missed him for all these years. She said how much she'd love to see him again, how much she longed to finally heal old wounds so they could become, in the winter of his life, a family again.

She sent it, and she waited.

A couple of days later, she received a call. Her father, she was told, had died that very afternoon. And in his mailbox sat her card, unopened.

The One-Eyed Jack

I originally intended to call this chapter "It's Never Too Late." *You always have a chance to make up for lost time*, I thought I'd say. *You always have a chance to be the father you could've and should've been. There's always that opportunity to make things better.*

But that's not true, is it? Not in this life anyway. Perhaps when we get to heaven we'll have a chance to talk with our loved ones — our sons and daughters, the fathers we never knew or never appreciated — and work it all out. We'll love each other like we should've loved before.

But here on earth, we have only a little time given to us. And none of us knows how long that time will be.

While the story of the woman and her father packs a punch, I doubt it's highly unusual. It may have unique details, but much of the rest sounds all too familiar. The distance, the pain, the regret. Fathers, when they get it right, mean the world to their children. But too often, there's a disconnect. A rebellious son or daughter. An unresponsive or abusive dad. Perhaps the blame lies with one person or another, but often there's plenty of blame to go around. And then, all at once or bit by bit, a relationship breaks. The tether of love gets severed.

Before Father's Day of 2012, I wrote a blog post asking our readers what they'd do if they could spend one last day with their dads. Their answers, at times, broke my heart.

"It's good to read all the comments and know there are/ were some good fathers," wrote T.J. "As for me, as harsh as it sounds, I wouldn't want another day with mine. What he did to me and my family has virtually destroyed the ones left behind. I'll be glad when Sunday has come and gone."

"I would love to spend one more day with my dad," said Deb. "He is a very difficult man, and we have not spoken in eight years. I am reaching out to him this Father's Day. If you read this, please pray my dad will have a soft, open, and receptive heart toward me. Thank you."

And then there was this from someone calling himself RiRL:

"I'd say, 'Hi, Dad. It's nice to finally meet you.'"

You don't hear about so many broken relationships with moms. Mothers don't fall down on the job quite as often. Oh, it can happen. But it doesn't happen nearly as often. More often than not, they're the ones to kiss the skinned knees, to slap on the Band-Aid, to help with the homework. If only one parent goes to a school play or pitches in on a field trip, it's probably the mother. According to a study published in *Social Forces* in 2008, moms, even working moms, were more likely to stay home with sick kids than dads were.[32] Single-parent households are far more likely to be headed by women than men.

Dads? They're the wild cards — the one-eyed Jacks that can either make or break a family's hand. All too often they break. The National Center for Fathering says that, in 2009, 39 percent of fathers never read to their kids, nearly a third never visited their child's classroom, and more than half admitted to never volunteering at their kids' school.[33] These trends have become so accepted that they're a sitcom cliché. Marge Simpson dotes on her kids while clueless Homer hides in Moe's Tavern. And while Homer may mean well, there's no question who Bart and Lisa will turn to if they really need help. Homer? Only a last resort.

According to the *Wall Street Journal*, in 2013 we Americans spent 41 percent more on Mother's Day than Father's Day.[34] Does that surprise anyone?

Some dads aren't just underinvolved with their kids' lives; they're uninvolved. And some children, like RiRL, never know their fathers at all.

Hi, Dad. It's nice to finally meet you.

A few lament the loss in online support groups like The Experience Project, and the stories have a poignant sense of repetition. It sounds as if they mourn a relationship they never had, a bond aborted before it could form.

- I am twenty-three years old and all my life my toxic family told me that my real father knew that I existed, knew that I belonged to him ... but wanted nothing to do with me ...

- The only time I ever saw my father was ... for my [first] birthday party. I have always told myself that I am mad/indifferent ...

- I'm fourteen years old and I never met my real father ...

- I am a thirty-five-year-old who has never met his father ...

- I am a sixteen-year-old girl who had to grow up not knowing a single thing about who my father was ...

Fathers can break their kids' hearts, even if they never know them. In just a few short minutes, a man can become a father. But so many don't realize what being a father is or what it means. Do some regret it? Maybe. But how many try to repair the bonds they broke? Patch up those relationships that never were? Meet the children who for years, maybe decades, have yearned to talk with and understand and maybe even love their father?

They don't know what they're missing. They toss the bonds aside like a scratched-up lottery ticket, not understanding that they own a winner. That being a dad, a good dad, makes a Powerball jackpot look puny.

And that's why it's so important for you and me to never waste a week, a day, or a minute. We should never let a moment slip by when we can show our kids that we love them.

On one level, it *is* never too late. It's never too late to love your children. It's never too late to teach them. It's never too late to give them the care and attention that only a father can give. But that word *never* comes with an asterisk. When you read the fine print, you find that you don't have all the time in the world to grow those bonds and make things right. The task calls for a little urgency, a little effort. Make the most of every day because you don't know how many days you have together.

Spending One More Day

Those moments become monuments in our kids' memories, landmarks they can hold on to for the rest of their lives. Make moments, I tell you. When I look over some of those responses to my 2012 Father's Day blog post, the importance of those moments gets confirmed time and time again.

How would these blog readers spend one more day with their dads?

"I always admired him for how he either knew or could figure out how to fix almost anything," wrote Susan. "I'd like to work with him on a project."

"One of my most treasured memories growing up was going camping with my family," Nanci said. "My favorite part was taking a walk from the campsite with my dad. You had his full attention and didn't have to share him with anyone else."

This from Stephos: "If I could spend one more day with my dad, I'd take him to an Eagles concert and sing every single song with him at the top of my lungs. And then I'd thank God for the chance to say good-bye to him."

Moment after moment found its way into the comments section. Some would dance with their fathers or listen to them play the ukulele. They'd bake together or drive a beat-up pickup around the farm. They'd fish. They'd golf. They'd see a baseball game or play Scrabble. Almost every moment replayed one of their favorite childhood memories, a time when they felt closer to their fathers than anyone else in the world.

And most often, people said they'd just want to talk with Dad again. They wanted to hear their father's voice roll through the air one more day, spinning stories or telling jokes. Some wanted to hear old, familiar family tales. Others wanted to hear things they never had a chance to hear before — stories about his childhood or about what he did in the war. "I wish I had one more day to talk to him about his life and his dreams and share our love of Jesus together," said a woman named Sherri. "After almost fifty years, I still miss him terribly."

Going Deep

I think that last comment reveals a lot, and it found an echo in many of the comments I read. *I wish I had one more day to talk to him about his life and his dreams and share our love of Jesus together.* She wanted to hear about him and what he considered most important.

How many of us dads miss *that* boat? How many of us pour so much of ourselves into our kids that we forget to actually *talk* with them about important things? We can read stories to them, build birdhouses with them, take them to ball games, and build all sorts of wonderful memories. And then, when they leave home, how many don't really know who we are? What's important to us?

I'm a big believer in doing. Make moments. Take risks. Teach in action. But those moments should involve conversation too — meaningful conversation. The moments we create for our kids take shape not only out of what we do but through what we say.

Jesus is a tremendous role model for us here (as in all things). Scripture portrays him as a Man of action. He heals the sick and walks on water and turns over tables in the temple, and in the end gets crucified on a cross. The Gospels are filled with accounts of what Jesus does.

But very often, those very actions stick in our minds not just because of what he did but also because of what he said as he did them.

When he encounters a paralyzed man, Jesus first forgives the man's sins. And when he finds that people question him, Jesus decides to reveal a portion of his character: "Which is easier," he asks — "to say to this paralyzed man, 'Your sins are forgiven,' or to say, 'Get up, take your mat and walk'? But I want you to know that the Son of Man has authority on earth to forgive sins." And so Jesus said to the man, "I tell you, get up, take your mat and go home" (Mark 2:9 – 11).

And the paralyzed man did just that.

"You of little faith," Jesus tells Peter after walking on water. "Why did you doubt?" (Matthew 14:31).

When Jesus overturned the tables and benches in the temple courts, he hollered, "It is written … 'My house will be called a house of prayer,' but you are making it 'a den of robbers'" (Matthew 21:13), leaving no question as to why he got so angry.

And while on the cross, Jesus cried out, "Father, forgive them, for they do not know what they are doing" (Luke 23:34), revealing his boundless mercy for those who deserved it least.

In truth, Jesus was remarkable not just because of his deeds (as amazing as they were). If we were to know only what he *did*, we'd think of him as a very impressive miracle worker. But the Bible tells of plenty of miracle workers. It's through Jesus' *words* that we came to know him as the Son of God.

Likewise, our kids get to know us through our words and, by extension, more of who they are as well. Through talking, we tell them a little of our own stories and where they came from. They learn they're not just a blip on the screen but part of a story — sometimes beautiful, sometimes sad, often a little of both. A story that has been told and retold for generations. Through these talks, we teach our children what we consider important. We can offer words of encouragement and love.

Dads, at least traditionally, aren't always good with words. Sometimes we struggle in this area because of how our parents raised us or how we were taught to think about what a man *should* be — John Wayne or James Caviezel, the strong, silent type. Sometimes we clam up because we fear what our children will say or think of us if we start speaking. So we stick with safer subjects. We stick with news, weather, and sports, subjects that may seem interesting today but will have very little relevance a couple of years from now, or even a couple of weeks from now. "You hear about the new Costco opening up?" "Wow, check out those clouds — looks like rain." "Man, can you believe how the Rockies got pounded last night?" We choose light subjects. Innocuous. Superficial. Mere sound to fill the space.

But our kids long for more.

Dad, what do you feel? they wonder. *What's in your heart? I need to know because I want to know if what I'm feeling is right or wrong.*

When someone close to us dies, what do we often regret? What we left unsaid. "I'm sorry." "I'm proud of you." "I love you."

The words come easy — so why do we find it so hard to say them? Why does it seem so hard to talk to our family about things that matter, things that can matter to them *and* to you?

News, weather, and sports. You know, I'm not above that. In fact, I kind of thrive on that. I know a lot about the news, and I love my sports. Get me talking about football, and I'll talk your ear off. I have fun with those conversations. But man, when you can get past the headlines with your kids and dive deep — when you can get into an important discussion about things that matter more than the go-ahead touchdown in a Vikings-Bears game — it's so much more fun. It transcends the conversation itself and becomes a moment. And you can almost see their minds blossoming.

If you find it hard to talk with your children, ponder this advice: In a moment when you feel creative and think of things you'd like to discuss with your kids, write them down. Jot down three or four things you'd like to ask your son or daughter on an index card. Put it in your pocket. You might not even need to refer to it, but it'll remind you that the next time you're with your child, you have something to ask them. And then just do it. "You know, Julie, I wanted to ask you a question."

Kids tend to understand the importance of talks like this so much better than adults do. We get so blurry and busy. But children seem to understand almost innately the preciousness and sacredness of life. We sometimes mistakenly think that kids see life as just a game. They don't know what work is or how to be serious. But for kids, the very games they play *are* serious. They're important in that moment, as important as anything. Kids feel the value of time, even if they don't understand it. They feel the beauty of life and of nature, even if they don't put terms to it. And when they experience pain, they hurt just as much or more than we adults do.

Ask a child a really deep question, and they'll get it. They'll think about it and take it seriously.

It's better to start these conversations when they're young, of course. It makes the questions easier as they get older. But it's when they get older, maybe thirteen or fourteen, that they'll appreciate it the most. When you ask them something deep, they'll think about it. They'll feel grateful that you asked, that you think enough of them to take them seriously. And most importantly, they'll feel that much more connected to you. You'll strengthen another thread to that bond, that tether of love, between you.

And maybe, most importantly, when they have a question —a serious, heartfelt question—they won't hesitate to ask you or come to you for advice. They'll invite you to speak into their life. And what's more special than that?

Even when you grow old and your kids are all grown-up,

it's never too late to talk to them. As long as we live, it's never too late.

Food for Thought

My dad and I never had a chance to talk with each other. He didn't know how. And for a long time maybe he didn't want to. His booze took first place for so long. His kids became almost an afterthought. And as the last-born of five, I was *definitely* an afterthought.

When I moved back in with him, I think he wanted to be a real dad to me. He wanted to make up for some of what had happened before — the hammer night for sure, the baseball mitt he told me he'd bring me but never did. I think, in a way, he wanted to start over. Maybe he thought it wasn't too late to become a real father to me. A good dad.

But he still didn't know how, really. He was nearly seventy by then. I was eleven. He didn't know how to talk to me. Outside of baseball, he didn't know what I cared about. He had no clue about my hopes or my fears. And he didn't, or couldn't, ask.

So he showed his affection the only way he really could — he cooked me breakfast. Every weekend, he cooked for the two of us. The eggs would be sunny-side-up and the bacon often a little burnt, and he'd serve the toast slathered in peanut butter.

One Saturday morning, I climbed out of bed and followed the smell of bacon into the kitchen. My dad had finished cooking. He tossed the bacon and eggs onto a plate and slid it in front of me. I noticed a little stream of yellow coming from the eggs.

"I can't eat this," I announced. "The eggs are all runny."

My dad, for all of his problems, never hit me. Never. But on that Saturday morning I saw his anger flare in a way I hadn't seen it in years, not since the night of the hammer. He walked over to me and raised his hand as if he were going to slap me. And then he checked himself.

"You're so ungrateful," he said. And then he walked away.

I sat there staring at my eggs and bacon and peanut butter toast, and I knew in my heart he was right. *That's true*, I thought. *I am being ungrateful. I'm not living with the Reils anymore.*

It felt like a little bell went off in my head. Until that moment, part of me thought of hurt as a one-way street — my fathers always caused me pain. I never understood, until that morning, that I could hurt my father too.

Pain's a Part of Relationship

"You always hurt the one you love," the old song goes, and it's sadly true. The moments will come when you hurt your kids. You'll say something you shouldn't have. You'll do something that embarrasses them. You'll break a promise. None of us are perfect. And even when we say we're sorry and admit our faults, we can't erase what happened.

Our kids can hurt us too, sometimes accidentally and sometimes on purpose. They can lie. They can scream insults. They can slam doors or smash things or even hit us. And when they get older, sometimes the hurts can grow far worse. They can rebel. They can reject everything we tried to teach them. They can get into drugs or alcohol or promiscuity, and we'll feel powerless to help or protect them.

When we look at the Bible, we see a depressing number of hurting families and grieving fathers. How grieved would Isaac feel when he learned that Jacob had tricked him and stolen his brother's birthright? How many nights did the father of the prodigal son wonder, with a heavy heart, whether his boy was safe or even alive? I think about David grieving over his rebellious son, Absalom, after his boy died. "O my son Absalom! My son, my son Absalom!" he cried over and over (2 Samuel 18:33). I wonder: Did he grieve much less when Absalom forced his own father out of Jerusalem? Wouldn't every father grieve?

This all brings us back to the importance of making moments with our children. These moments serve so many purposes. They're memories to cherish. They're teaching opportunities. They're fun. But most importantly, they're monuments that father and child alike can hold on to, monuments to your love and reminders of those bonds of affection that tie father and child together and keep them forever connected.

We can't forget that, whatever the hurt or the wound, love really does conquer all. Love is irresistible, irrefutable, undeniable. Nothing rises to it. The dark side of our character has no weapon against it. It's our trump card, and I think it's the only one we have in the deck. Love is the key. That tether of love is the key to everything.

The tether of love, if you have rebellious children, becomes paramount to your relationship. Your kids can irritate you, frustrate you, and drive you to stop talking to them. That tether can fray, and fray badly, in the heat of anger, hurt, and heartache. But you can't allow those frustrations to overwhelm your love. You must hold on to those moments you've built. You have to hang on to that tether, even if it's just a thread. Because when your rebellious son or daughter turns twenty or twenty-five or thirty, they may remember those moments and long to see you and hear your voice and maybe even say they're sorry. If that thread exists, they can find it and follow it back to you. They know that, despite how much they hurt you and disappointed you and damaged their relationship with you, the thread of love continues to exist. They see it. They know the tether has never completely snapped. And then the two of you can begin to make some new moments, some new threads, to strengthen that bond once again.

To Forgive Is Divine (And Very, Very Hard)

But what happens if the tether breaks? What if the relationship gets truly severed? Is it too late then? Is there truly no hope?

There *is* hope, I believe. It's never too late — as long as both father and child are still living.

But I don't want to think simplistically about the process. If the tether breaks, it's very, very difficult to tie it back together. And forgiveness has to come in torrents. If our love is a tether, then forgiveness is the knot that can mend the two pieces back together. If we don't have someone willing to forgive, and sometimes forgive a lot, we don't have a lot of hope, in my opinion.

But here's the good news: If we do have forgiveness in such situations, then I think the tether can wind up even stronger than before.

We see it often in marriages when a serious failure or breach of trust has occurred — lying, adultery, or any number of behaviors. Once everything has come out in the open, those involved in the relationship may be able to save it and even strengthen it. Renewed honesty allows the level of trust to rise. Forgiveness from one party can boost gratitude from the other. Where there is trust and gratitude, the love and affection two people have for each other can grow again — even stronger and in deeper and healthier ways.

It seems counterintuitive, but I see it time and time again. Couples who fight through those situations come out on the other side healthier and even happier. And now they have nothing to hide. It again reflects that simple truth Paul outlined in his letter to the Romans — suffering can lead to hope.

In the same way, honesty and forgiveness can heal relationships between fathers and their children. But man, it can be hard to forgive! It's much easier to bury our hurt in a pile of complacency and fool ourselves (or pretend) that we've forgiven. Forgiveness doesn't come easy to us. It's not natural. Revenge is easy, while forgiveness comes primarily through faith, by the strength that comes through Jesus. Anytime you say, "I've forgiven you," even if you say it in your own mind, you should question yourself: Have you really forgiven this person? Or have you simply turned your heart off to the pain? A good test to know your true feelings is to imagine if something happened to the person you've "forgiven." If they died or were seriously injured, what would you feel? Joy? Pain? Indifference? That little test can provide a view into your own heart.

Sometimes what we call forgiveness is really nothing more than a mask, one more tool we use to hide the pain from others and ourselves. Forgiveness is hard. I struggle with it to this day.

I don't hold grudges. If I saw Hank or Mr. Reil today, I'd shake their hands. But have I truly forgiven my failed fathers? Or do I just not care anymore?

I think I have forgiven my father. I found that path to forgiveness easier, because I knew he loved me. While in many ways he was a horrific father, I still felt his love. And even as a child, I could distinguish between his love and his mistakes.

I think I've forgiven Mr. Reil, just because I feel sorry for him, a sad, confused man. Perhaps what he did to me wasn't exactly his fault. And in a way, perhaps that means I have nothing to forgive. You don't forgive the rain for ruining your picnic or for flooding your basement. I saw no malice or purpose to Mr. Reil's fear of me. He didn't know reality. I just felt sorry for him because a grown man should know better, and he didn't.

But if I'm being honest with myself, I doubt I've forgiven Hank. At times it feels as if I have, but disregard is not forgiveness. I don't care, just as he may never really have cared for me. It's sad to say that, and I'm embarrassed to say it, but I think it's true. Hank is in God's hands. But emotionally I can't expend the time.

About a year ago, I visited my mom's gravesite — the first time I'd gone there since I was ten. Hank had bought two adjoining plots when Mom died, one for her and one for him. He imagined at the time, I suppose, that the two of them could lie there side by side until the world stopped spinning.

I expected to see Hank there too, beside my mom as he imagined. I hadn't seen him since the day of the funeral, and I braced to "see" him, albeit in a much different form, for the first time in forty years. Maybe for the last time.

I remembered as I walked to the grave his last words he ever spoke to us: "I can't deal with this." And when I got to the gravesite, those words struck me anew. In front of me lay more evidence.

A stranger — some other woman — now lies beside my mother's body. Hank must've sold the gravesite. He ran away from us, and in the end he ran away from her. He scrubbed us all clean from his life.

I don't know if he's alive or dead. I do wonder, though, whether he ever looked back on those two years he spent with my mom and wondered if he could've, should've, done things differently. Could he have become a better stepfather? Did he have it in him even to try? Did he ever feel regret? Did he ever have the urge to find us again, to call one of us Daly kids and apologize? Or, for him, was it just too late?

It's Never Too Late

I know I'm not alone in wondering. Some men reading this book live with the pain of a damaged relationship. Others still wake up with a hurt inside them. Maybe they had a hard relationship with their own father, a story that sounds a little like mine. Maybe their dad drank too much or abused drugs or doled out abuse. Maybe he was a workaholic. Maybe he landed in jail. And the pain, after all this time, lingers.

Maybe you hurt your father. You left home in a huff, turned your back on your dad and family and went as far away as you could. And now that you have children of your own, you long to reconnect, but you don't know how.

Maybe I have some readers like Hank. They never took the time to know their children. Perhaps they've never even seen them. But sometimes they wonder about them. *Do they have families of their own? Have they moved on?* They wish they could've done things differently. But they wonder — is it too late?

It's never too late, not as long as we have breath in our bodies. Our relationships may have bent. They may even have broken. But with time and effort and a whole lot of forgiveness, we can mend them. There is hope! There's still a chance to make a moment or two. Or twenty. Or two hundred. There's still a chance to reconnect with your father.

There's still a chance to be a good dad.

The Light of Love

I once heard a story about a woman who hated her father.

Author and speaker Rob Parsons tells this one, about a girl who ran away from home when she was fifteen. She left in a huff and never thought she'd darken her parents' door again.

And for years she didn't.

But some nights, especially on nights near Christmas, she'd find herself driving down her old street and looking at her house, the Christmas tree sparkling in the window, the porch light glimmering in the dusk as if to welcome any who approached. That light always seemed to stay on.

The girl dared not go in. She couldn't. Too much had happened between her and her parents. But the porch light continued to twinkle, reminding her of better times, of moments she'd shared with her mother and father. And inevitably, she'd spend Christmas Eve parked on that street, across from her parents' house, somehow comforted by the little yellow porch light.

Then one year, the girl, now a woman, got tired of spending Christmas Eve in the car. She decided to take a risk. She decided to go home. And, of course, she received a grand welcome, like the prodigal child, with arms open wide to draw her close.

As she hugged her mother in the doorway, the woman talked about the porch light and how it had always seemed to remain on, no matter when she'd drive by.

Her mother smiled. "You know," she said, her eyes filled with tears, "I always left that light on for you. Just in case you came home."

Home. It's what we as fathers strive to create. It's what we build; it's what we protect. Home is the stories we tell, the lessons we teach, the moments we make. Home is family. Home is one of the most precious things we have.

It's time for us all to come home. It's time to make a home. It's not too late.

─────────── **TO THINK ABOUT** ───────────

1. If you could have another day with your father, how would you spend it? If your father is still alive, is it possible to have that day with him now?

2. How would you like to be remembered by your children? If you died today, how do you think they'd remember you?

3. Are there some specific things you'd like to tell your children? Questions you'd like to ask them? What are they?

4. Are there people in your life you should forgive? What can you do to speak or show your forgiveness to them? Can you identify people you should ask to forgive you?

Eleven

The Greatest of Joys

IN AUGUST 2013, *TIME* MAGAZINE RELEASED AN ISSUE WITH a cover that trumpeted "The Childfree Life: When Having It All Means Not Having Children." Reporter Lauren Sandler noted that the birthrate in the United States has reached the lowest level ever recorded. One in every five women, according to a Pew Research study cited by Sandler, leaves their child-bearing years without having borne a single child, up from one in ten when I grew up in the 1970s.[35]

Sandler talked with a number of women who chose to remain childless and who seem, more or less, content. "I do all sorts of things," says Jenna Johnson in the article. "Buy an unnecessary beautiful object, plan trips with our aging parents, sleep in, send care packages to nieces and nephews, enroll in language classes."

A bevy of other stories published online accompanied the story, including one by Beth Lapides, who declares in her headline, "I Just Don't Want a Child."[36]

"Not having kids is saying one big no," she writes. "No to the same thing over and over and over. So that you can say yes to everything else. I picked one big no and a million little yeses."

Obviously, the decision to have a child is a very personal one. Jean and I took some time to make this decision ourselves. I was nearly forty when Trent came into our lives, and I don't want to belittle the choices made by others on whether to start a family.

But even so, I found the cover story quite sad, even disturbing, for two reasons.

First, the attitude of some of the story's sources perplexed me. Some of them seemed to believe that to feel truly fulfilled, you can't have children. These people seem to say that the joy of having kids isn't worth the sacrifice. Frankly, I find that to be a pretty selfish attitude. God has given us the power to create life. And some apparently think this power, this *gift*, is no big deal. "Eh, who cares?" these people seem to say. "Not worth my time."

Second, it struck me how little attention the cover story, indeed, the whole collection of articles, paid to men. Almost all the sources Sandler quoted were women. Even online, *Time* published just one story written by a guy. And that guy, sociologist Philip Cohen, made it in because of his role as a demographer, not as someone either accepting or rejecting the challenge of fatherhood.

Others also noticed the testosterone vacuum in *Time*'s coverage. "Wouldn't it be grand if *Time* remembered that having children — or not having them — isn't something that only happens to women?" wrote Mary Elizabeth Williams on Salon.com.[37]

It's pretty discouraging, particularly at a time when we understand more than ever the importance of dads, to see a story relating to parenthood almost completely ignore the role of the father. Simple biology tells us you need a man and a woman to make a baby. Study after study has documented the positive influence dads can have on their kids and the serious damage that can result when they're not in the picture. Experts talk about a "fatherhood crisis." Political leaders from the left and right exhort men to take seriously their responsibilities as dads. And yet, in a huge think piece published in a major newsmagazine, it seems that only one voice, the voice of the woman, is worthy of attention and has relevance for the decision on whether to start a family. Men are an afterthought, if even that.

Time probably didn't intend the oversight, which to me makes it all the more troubling. It tells me that dads, culturally speaking, don't matter much. Since everyone knows they won't take much of an interest in the family, why should we bother to ask them anything? We so heartily embrace the stereotype of the uninvolved father — the sperm donor who cuts and runs, the alcoholic who sees his family in a boozy blur, the workaholic who doesn't have time for his kids — that sometimes we don't even ask him why he decided *not* to become a father.

Kids get in the way of happiness. Dads don't matter.

What a couple of lies.

Dads *do* matter. I hear about how much they matter every day at work when I talk with guests on the radio about their own families; when I read studies that illustrate their influence; when I hear the stories from our wide-ranging Focus family on how dads impacted their own homes. I see how much they matter at night when I come home and give my own boys big hugs and listen to them talk about how their day went.

And kids getting in the way of our happiness? It's just the opposite. They can provide the greatest joys in our lives. Perhaps we don't have, as Jenna Johnson says, the money to buy "an unnecessary beautiful object." That cash goes to braces and ballet lessons. Perhaps we don't have time to enroll in language classes; we're too busy making sure our kids learn proper English. But when our children walk for the first time or laugh at our jokes or bring us delight in ways that we can't quantify, we know that kids don't stand in the way of our happiness. Very often, they're the source of it.

With all due respect to Beth Lapides, to say yes to children doesn't mean submission to "the same thing over and over and over." It's the introduction to eighteen to twenty years of endless variety. Through our children, we can look at the miracle of God's creation through young eyes again — to see the world in all its wonder. We share life and engage with it in ways we'd never imagined.

When we say yes to fatherhood, we don't shut doors; we open them.

The Cost of Fatherhood

Of course, fans of childlessness do have a point. Some of those doors we open when we become fathers aren't all that fun to step through. All that joy comes with pain and stress and just plain ick. Sometimes the trip to the zoo comes with a tantrum. Sometimes that fantastic fireside chat precedes a kid vomiting in the tent. Raising kids comes with a cost. It's not fun all the time, and it can seem particularly costly when the time comes to balance the checkbook.

According to the United States Department of Agriculture, couples who gave birth to a child in 2012 can expect to spend $241,080 on that child by the time he or she is eighteen years old.[38] If you plan to send your child to college, ratchet that up a bit. In 2030, tuition for a private college could hover around $130,000 *a year*.[39]

And that says nothing about the other costs of parenthood — those frustrations and pains we suffer along the way. The late-night feedings and messy diapers. The screaming in the grocery store and uncomfortable conferences with teachers. The report cards. The fights. The sometimes sleepless nights. Parenthood isn't for wimps. Fatherhood, I've said, is all about sacrifice.

But in my mind, sacrifice makes parenthood so worthwhile.

"Do nothing out of selfish ambition or vain conceit. Rather, in humility value others above yourselves," Paul writes to the Philippians, "not looking to your own interests but each of you to the interests of the others" (Philippians 2:3 – 4).

Country singer Randy Travis put this philosophy a different way in his song "Three Wooden Crosses": "I guess it's not what you take when you leave this world behind you. It's what you leave behind you when you go."

God has commissioned us to look beyond ourselves and our own selfish desires — the stuff we buy and the language lessons we take — and consider the needs of others. And we should remain especially aware of our children's needs. The time and money we spend, and the patience and care we show, with our children are investments, ones that pay huge returns. Perhaps those returns don't always register on an economic spreadsheet. But fathers know the value.

And when the time comes to depart this world, what's going to be important to us? What we accumulated? Our many beautiful little things? What we accomplished? Perhaps that stuff matters a little. But far more important to us will be what we leave behind. What are your kids like? What sort of character do they have? What sort of lives do they lead? Those are the important things. Those are the things that make sense.

In 2013, scientists conducted a study that tried to quantify the importance of "happiness" and "meaning" to our overall health.[40] Often, of course, happiness and meaning go hand in hand. But for the study, scientists paid particular attention to what I might call *meaningless* happiness, defined in the study (published by the Proceedings of the National Academy of Sciences) as a "relatively shallow, self-absorbed or even selfish life, in which things go well, needs and desire are easily satisfied, and difficult or taxing entanglements are avoided."

Though lots of studies have shown that stress and unhappiness can cause health problems, these researchers found that happy people who live relatively meaningless lives are, in some ways, less healthy than those who live meaningful lives but don't feel as happy. The complicated explanation goes something like this: Genes in people living happy but hedonistic lives act as if they face constant adversity. That, in turn, fires up the body to fight bacterial infection, which primes cells for inflammation. This sort of pro-inflammatory stance, doctors have learned, has a connection with some very serious conditions, including heart disease and some types of cancer. But subjects who report lives of deeper meaning, even if they don't feel as happy, typically lack those problems.

All of which means that people who live *for fun* might have more health issues than people who have something to live *for*.

But scientists also point out that people who live meaningful lives often live very happy lives too, even if those lives don't seem as easy as others. Meaning not only makes us healthier; it can make us happier. Who doesn't like to have a reason to get out of bed in the morning?

God's design for our lives just plain works. He asks us to

live lives of meaning, after all — to live for others and not for ourselves. And so he designed us to operate best when we do what he wants us to do. When we look at the holistic nature of his plan, we don't see him standing off in a corner, dealing with just our spiritual well-being. He has an all-encompassing prescription for us. When we live lives of service and sacrifice — when we live *fulfilled* lives — we gain all these benefits because of how he wired us.

I remember walking down the road with my dad when I was a very young boy. I was wearing shorts and probably looking every bit a part of my Irish ancestry, with my pale skin and freckles everywhere. My dad looked down at me, and it felt like he saw me for the first time.

"Where'd ya get all those freckles?" he asked.

I looked down at my bare legs. "I guess God gave them to me," I told him, even though we never talked about God in my family. Even at that stage of my life I had an idea that some things come from God. And now that I'm older, I *know* that's true. Who and what we are come to us as gifts from his hand (even if they don't always seem like gifts). He made us this way.

God made men to be fathers. And when we embrace that reality, that gift, we find not just new ways to spend money and stress out but new happiness as well. New meaning. In a way, new life.

In some respects, good dads live for their children. We give them the best of us — our hopes, our principles, our experience, our love — and ask them to carry it with honor, to pass on those teachings to their children and to their children's children. This is how God made us. To be a good dad isn't just something we *should* do; it's something we were *built* to do. And because he designed us in this way, we're bound to love it when we try it. How could it be any other way?

Guiding Principles

My own fathers and father figures never understood what a life of meaning looked like. They never got the concept of sacrificing for their kids. Or if they did, they couldn't follow through. They never saw the joy in fatherhood. They saw only the stress and the burdensome responsibility. And so, in their own ways, they all ran or hid. They couldn't handle it.

But that made me all the more determined to be a good dad to my kids. I wanted to be the father I never had. Instead of leaving my children with memories of a drunken or distant dad, I want to give them moments to treasure and hold on to. My dads always seemed to leave when I needed them most. So I want to make sure my boys know I'm always there for them, even as I still give them opportunities to build perseverance, character, and hope. I want to be that voice of comfort and source of strength in their lives. I want to give them the solid, supporting old oak tree that I so much longed for as a child. I want them to know I will always strive to strengthen the tether of love connecting us.

And, when they're all grown up, I want them to take away a few basic principles to live with — things that will help give them lives filled with meaning.

The first thing I want to leave them with, of course, is a rock-solid commitment to Christ. This is critical. Ultimately, showing them how to walk with the Lord in this life is job one. Jean and I work on this job every day, setting in place the foundations of faith — the stories, the theology, the importance of trusting Jesus in every aspect of one's life. And we reinforce that groundwork every chance we get.

But there's more to it than that. It also means letting Trent and Troy know that times will come when they'll struggle with faith. We all go through periods like that — or at least most of us do.

I don't see Jean talking in quite the same way with the boys as I do. I don't know whether it's a male-female thing, but part of me suspects it might be. Dads sometimes feel the world's temptations more intensely. This helps explain why men seem much more erratic in relationships, while women tend to have more stability. Sure, we're all susceptible to sin and temptation and spiritual stumbling, but dads know where their hearts truly are and where they sometimes wander off. And because of that, maybe we understand the shortcomings in our own kids a little better.

So as Jean reinforces with our children the importance of walking the right path, I see my role as coming alongside and saying, "Yeah, definitely do that — but the times will come when you'll feel tempted to step off that path. And when that temptation comes, or even if you do step off, God is still with you. God still loves you. And God will be there to help you get back on track."

The second key principle I'm trying to give Trent and Troy is a sense of integrity. It's so important to be a trustworthy person. The Bible reinforces that fact in verse after verse, passage after passage. So whenever an opportunity comes up (those rare times when our kids bend the truth or cheat or engage in some other form of misbehaving), we talk about integrity and its importance. Integrity, after all, isn't just about keeping Mom and Dad happy. It's about turning into a man whom others can trust. And so we won't just punish Trent or Troy for lying. We'll go deep with them. We'll walk them through their own process of discernment so they can better understand how important integrity is — and, I hope, give them tools to handle a similar situation better the next time around. "What motivated you to do that?" we'll ask. "Why did you feel you had to? Did you fear something? What would you do differently now that we've talked?" We do this so they'll understand how much better and, in some ways, easier it is to tell the truth from the beginning.

The third guiding principle is trying to teach our boys kindness and courtesy, how to treat people well — and why. This, too, is a critical principle because a sense of consideration and generosity is foundational to developing greater selflessness.

God calls us all to become as selfless as possible. "Love your enemies, do good to them, and lend to them without expecting to get anything back," Jesus teaches in Luke 6:35. "Then your reward will be great, and you will be children of the Most High, because he is kind to the ungrateful and wicked."

I doubt many of us arrive on earth as naturally selfless — Mother Teresa maybe, but after her the list gets pretty short. Generally, we are bent toward selfishness. This seems to be a particularly big challenge in the Daly family. God has blessed us, and we get to do a lot of fun things. Jean and I concentrate on telling our boys that not everyone gets to do some of the things we get to do, and that whenever we can, we need to act generously with what God has given us and be deeply considerate of everyone around us.

All of these principles interlock. If we take our relationship with God seriously, we'll want to become people of integrity and try to mirror Jesus' kindness and selflessness. To show integrity means to take not only your word seriously but also your relationships with both God and other people. True selflessness requires that we temper our own wishes, not just so we can help others, but so we can bend our knee to God and submit to his ideals.

At the core of all these principles, of course, lies love. We love Jesus and want to walk with him. Our love for God makes us want to become people of integrity and follow the design he laid out for us. And, of course, he calls us to love one another. Love is at the heart of it all.

And that's why, as we teach our own boys these lessons, we try to set each within the framework of love. Without love, all of these principles are meaningless. Without love, none of these lessons will take.

"If I speak in the tongues of men or of angels, but do not have love, I am only a resounding gong or a clanging cymbal," Paul writes in 1 Corinthians 13. "If I have the gift of prophecy and can fathom all mysteries and all knowledge, and if I have a faith that can move mountains, but do not have love, I am nothing. If I give all I possess to the poor and give over my body to hardship that I may boast, but do not have love, I gain nothing." Love is the key to everything we are and everything we do. And so we want love to be the foundation of every hug we give, every lesson we teach, and even every punishment we have to administer. We want to teach our boys the value of love and help them understand that the family is a safe place, a loving place, to learn all sorts of lessons. Jean does this especially well — amplifying this lesson and restating it over and over again.

Love is what family, and fatherhood, is all about.

Letting Go

Sometimes fathers find it hard to keep the big picture in mind while in the midst of raising their kids. Our job is to raise our kids to adulthood, to prepare them for the way ahead. But sometimes it can feel like a job that will never end. They'll *never* get out of diapers. They'll *never* stop banging on pots.

They'll *always* sass Mom or break curfew. It seems sometimes like they'll never grow up.

But then one day they do. They go off to college or get married. They move across town or to the other side of the world. They pack their bags, clean out their bedrooms, and wave good-bye.

And there will come a moment when you realize that, even though you'll always be a father, things will never be the same.

Maybe you realize it when you stand on the porch and watch him drive away, until his car becomes nothing but a speck on the horizon. Or you sit in the church pew, listening to your little girl say "I do" to another man. It could come when you take a walk around the block — a walk you had taken with them countless times — or watch a movie they used to love. It could come without warning, seemingly triggered by nothing at all.

The moments you've built with your child will rush back in a wave. You'll realize that you'd do almost anything to have more time with your kids, to hear them bang on pots one more time, to watch them ride their bikes in the yard. To talk with them. Teach them. Read to them. Hug them tight. To be that oak tree — the one they needed, the one they depended on — one more time.

But you know it's their turn now. They must take what you've taught them and use it to make a new life. And if you've been a good dad, you'll know you've given them the tools to do just that.

It reminds me of the final scenes from Steven Spielberg's 1998 film *Saving Private Ryan*. The titular character, Private James Ryan, is going to be sent home after his three brothers are killed in action. A small group of soldiers, led by Captain John Miller, must find the guy and save him. Eventually they succeed. But in the course of the mission, almost all of the men die, and Captain Miller lies mortally wounded, bleeding out beside Private Ryan. Miller, blood-soaked and pale, motions Ryan to come closer.

"James," he whispers, "earn this. Earn it."

As fathers, as good dads, we whisper the same thing to our children. "Earn it," we say. "Live a life of honor. Make it count for something."

But perhaps we're a little like Private Ryan too.

Decades later, Ryan stands in the middle of the Normandy American Cemetery, staring at the cross that marks the grave of Captain Miller. "Tell me I have lived a good life," he says to his wife. "Tell me I'm a good man."

And just as we exhort our children to live lives of honor, we fathers must examine ourselves. How we have invested in our kids. How we've measured up to give them the best possible foundation to go into the world. We ask ourselves, "Have I done my job? Have I been a good man? Have I been a good dad?"

Some men will never be able to say they've been good fathers. Instead of building strong foundations, they've cracked them. Instead of exhorting their children to live lives of honor and purpose, they say, in essence, "Go and do the best you can. Find meaning somewhere, because I haven't given it to you. Drill down if you can, because right now, you're on sand. I've given you nothing to build on.

"Get out," they say. "Go on. You're on your own."

A Life of Meaning

What is a good dad? How do we know we've been one? As we're raising our kids, it can sometimes seem hard to tell. And even when they're grown-up, it can seem tricky. At times you may wonder whether your child listened to you at all. Sometimes you may wonder whether all your hard work went for nothing.

In times like these, I hope you'll have your own moments to hold on to.

When Trent and I took our Adventures in Fatherhood retreat around Yosemite, there came a night when the children were supposed to honor and bless their fathers around the campfire, a formal expression of love and meaning.

Trent talked about how much he loves me. How much he knows I care for him and love him. And then as he wrapped up, he said this:

"My life would have no meaning without you as my father."

Boom. A moment.

We walked back to our little sleeping area, our sleeping bags under the stars, and he turned to me and said, "Dad, I did it all off the cuff! Some of the other boys, they were preparing things for their dads. But I thought I'd just tell you what I'm thinking."

Man, what a blessing he gave me. Incredible! It's a moment I'll hold on to forever — especially when Trent talks back or spends hours away with his friends or acts like the teenager he is. I'll never let go of that moment.

Being a good dad is all about moments — moments to teach, moments to treasure. It's about the hard moments when we think we haven't gotten through to our kids, and the wonderful moments when we realize we have. It's about the moments we fall and the moments we fail. Most importantly, it's about the moments we get back up on our feet and try again. It's about never wasting a moment with our children, about making sacrifices and showing our love. Always.

It's not easy being a good dad. Many men run the other way because it feels too hard and demanding. But those who don't run, those who turn and face their role as dad, discover that all the work, pain, and sacrifice was worth it. Because when we give of ourselves, we get so much in return. When we live for others, we experience a life worth living.

―――――――――― **TO THINK ABOUT** ――――――――――

1. If you're a father, what's the hardest part of your job? If you're not a dad yet, what do you imagine will be the hardest?

2. Are you teaching your children to walk with God? Are you teaching them integrity? Are you teaching them kindness? How?

3. "Tell me I have lived a good life," Private Ryan says. "Tell me I've been a good man." Can you tell yourself both of those things?

Acknowledgments

THIS BOOK SPEAKS FROM MY HEART ABOUT A TOPIC THAT HAS brought me both great pain (the pain of not having a good dad) and great joy (the joy of being a better one).

First, I want to acknowledge my family — my wonderful wife, Jean, my partner in parenthood, who is always patient with me, always understanding, always encouraging. And my two boys, Trent and Troy, the two most amazing wonders in my life. You have shown me how to be a better dad.

To Paul Asay, my collaborator, thank you for the many hours of talking, thinking, and organizing. You are a gifted writer and contemplative father. Thank you for your insights and partnership.

To the entire team at Zondervan, including (but not limited to) Dirk Buursma, Tom Dean, and, most especially, editor John Sloan, who believed in the project and encouraged me with his tears.

To Wes Yoder, my agent, who understands the hearts of men.

And, of course, to director of public relations Monica Schleicher and all those at Focus on the Family who helped make this book a reality through their advice, research, and time. Thank you to each of you for your contributions into my life and this book.

Notes

1. Cited in Luke Rosiak, "Fathers Disappear from Households across America," *Washington Times*, December 25, 2012, www.washingtontimes.com/news/2012/dec/25/fathers-disappear-from-households-across-america/?page=all (accessed November 7, 2013).

2. See National KIDS COUNT, "Children in Single-Parent Families by Race," http://datacenter.kidscount.org/data/tables/107-children-in-single-parent-families-by#detailed/1/any/false/867,133,38,35,18/10,168,9,12,1,13,185/432,431 (accessed November 7, 2013).

3. National Center for Fathering, "Fathering in America," May 2009 (National Fathering Survey), www.fathers.com/documents/research/2009_Fathering_in_America_Summary.pdf (accessed November 7, 2013).

4. National Fatherhood Initiative, "The Father Factor," www.fatherhood.org/media/consequences-of-father-absence-statistics (accessed November 7, 2013).

5. Ibid.

6. Ibid.

7. Kent Nerburn, *Letters to My Son: Reflections on Becoming a Man*, rev. ed. (Novato, CA: New World Library, 1999), 173.

8. Pew Research Center, "Most Say Being a Father Today Is More Difficult," June 12, 2012, www.pewresearch.org/daily-number/ most-say-being-a-father-today-is-more-difficult/ (accessed November 7, 2013).

9. United States Department of Labor, "Women in the Labor Force in 2010," www.dol.gov/wb/factsheets/Qf-laborforce-10.htm (accessed November 7, 2013).

10. Catherine Rampell, "Enrollment Drops Again in Graduate Programs," New York Times, September 28, 2012, www.nytimes .com/2012/09/28/business/new-enrollment-drops-again-in-us -graduate-schools.html?_r=0 (accessed November 7, 2013).

11. Cited in Kim Parker and Wendy Wang, "Modern Parenthood: Roles of Moms and Dads Converge as They Balance Work and Family," March 14, 2013, Pew Research Social & Demographic Trends, www.pewsocialtrends.org/2013/03/14/modern -parenthood-roles-of-moms-and-dads-converge-as-they -balance-work-and-family/ (accessed November 7, 2013).

12. W. S. Aquilino, "The Noncustodial Father-Child Relationship from Adolescence into Young Adulthood," Journal of Marriage and Family 68 (2006): 929 – 46.

13. "Men Respond More Aggressively Than Women to Stress and It's All Down to a Single Gene," ScienceDaily, March 8, 2012, www.sciencedaily.com/releases/2012/03/120308071058.htm (accessed November 7, 2013).

14. Gretchen Livingston, "The Rise of Single Fathers," July 2, 2013, Pew Research Social & Demographic Trends, www .pewsocialtrends.org/2013/07/02/the-rise-of-single-fathers/ (accessed November 7, 2013).

15. Ibid.

16. Jason Skoda, "Paul Moro Nears Win No. 300 as Blue Ridge Football Coach," September 27, 2012, MaxPreps, www .maxpreps.com/news/BeA1SH-B-0KSp-OQGIqEMw/paul -moro-nears-win-no-300-as-blue-ridge-football-coach.htm (accessed November 7, 2013).

17. Aleksandr Solzhenitsyn, *The Gulag Archipelago*, vol. 1 (1973; repr., New York: HarperCollins, 2007), 186.

18. Tony Evans, *Kingdom Man* (Downers Grove, IL: Tyndale, 2012), 7.

19. Kyle Pruett and Marsha Kline Pruett, *Partnership Parenting* (Cambridge, MA: Da Capo Press, 2009), 100.

20. Cited in Kendra Cherry, "Parenting Style: The Four Styles of Parenting," http://psychology.about.com/od/developmental psychology/a/parenting-style.htm (accessed November 7, 2013).

21. Cited in Binyamin Appelbaum, "Study of Men's Falling Income Cites Single Parents," *New York Times*, March 20, 2013, www.nytimes.com/2013/03/21/business/economy/as-men -lose-economic-ground-clues-in-the-family.html (accessed November 7, 2013).

22. National Center for Fathering, "Fathering in America," May 2009 (National Fathering Survey), www.fathers.com/ documents/research/2009_Fathering_in_America_Summary .pdf (accessed November 7, 2013).

23. Child Welfare Information Gateway, "Domestic Violence and the Child Welfare System," www.childwelfare.gov/pubs/ factsheets/domestic_violence/impact.cfm (accessed November 7, 2013).

24. National Coalition Against Domestic Violence, "Domestic Violence Facts," www.ncadv.org/files/DomesticViolence FactSheet(National).pdf (accessed November 7, 2013).

25. Ibid.

26. Daily Mail Reporter, " 'She Is My Heart and I Am Her Legs': Devoted Dad Runs Triathlon Carrying His Teenager Daughter with Cerebral Palsy Because She Loves Being Outdoors," *MailOnline*, August 14, 2012, www.dailymail.co.uk/news/ article-2188373/Rick-van-Beek-Devoted-dad-runs-triathlon- carrying-teenager-daughter-cerebral-palsy.html (accessed November 7, 2013).

27. Teammaddy1, "Blog 1," *YouTube*, www.youtube.com/watch
?v=m2l-m7HtxJc (accessed November 7, 2013).

28. Ibid.

29. Mental Health America, "Depression in Teens," www.nmha
.org/index.cfm?objectid=C7DF950F-1372-4D20-C8B5BD8
DFDD94CF1 (accessed November 7, 2013).

30. Centers for Disease Control and Prevention, "Suicide
Prevention: Youth Suicide," http://www.cdc.gov/violence
prevention/pub/youth_suicide.html (accessed November 7,
2013).

31. Elizabeth Mendes, "In U.S., Optimism About Future for
Youth Reaches All-Time Low," May 2, 2011, www.gallup.com/
poll/147350/Optimism-Future-Youth-Reaches-Time-Low
.aspx (accessed November 7, 2013); see also Catherine Rampell,
"Dimming Optimism for Today's Youth," *New York Times*,
May 2, 2011, http://economix.blogs.nytimes.com/2011/05/02/
dimming-optimism-for-todays-youth/ (accessed November 7,
2013).

32. David J. Maume, "Gender Differences in Providing Urgent
Childcare among Dual-earner Parents," *Social Forces* 87.1
(2008): 273 – 97.

33. National Center for Fathering and National PTA, "Survey
of Father's Involvement in Children's Learning: Summary of
Study Findings," May 2009, www.fathers.com/documents/
research/2009_Education_Survey_Summary.pdf (accessed
November 7, 2013).

34. Phil Izzo, "Number of the Week: Americans Spend 41% More
on Mom Than Dad," *Wall Street Journal*, June 15, 2013, http://
blogs.wsj.com/economics/2013/06/15/number-of-the-week
-americans-spend-41-more-on-mom-than-dad/ (accessed
November 7, 2013).

35. Lauren Sandler, "Having It All Without Having Children,"
Time, August 12, 2013, http://content.time.com/time/magazine/
article/0,9171,2148636,00.html (accessed November 7, 2013).

36. Beth Lapides, "I Just Don't Want a Child," *Time*, August 1, 2013, http://ideas.time.com/2013/08/01/i-just-dont-want-a-child/ (accessed November 7, 2013).

37. Mary Elizabeth Williams, "Time Discovers Some People Don't Have Kids," *Salon*, August 1, 2013, www.salon.com/2013/08/01/ time_discovers_some_people_dont_have_kids/ (accessed November 7, 2013).

38. United States Department of Agriculture, "Parents Projected to Spend $241,080 to Raise a Child Born in 2012, According to USDA," www.usda.gov/wps/portal/usda/ usdahome?contentid=2013/08/0160.xml (accessed November 7, 2013).

39. Stephanie Landsman, "What College Tuition Will Look Like in 18 Years," *CNBC*, May 12, 2012, www.cnbc.com/id/47565202 (accessed November 7, 2013).

40. Emily Esfahani Smith, "Meaning Is Healthier Than Happiness," *The Atlantic*, August 1, 2013, www.theatlantic.com/health/ archive/2013/08/meaning-is-healthier-than-happiness/278250/ (accessed November 7, 2013).

ReFocus

Living a Life that Reflects God's Heart

Jim Daly, President of Focus on the Family, with Paul Batura

Jim Daly, the compassionate leader of Focus on the Family, inspires Christians to transcend political agendas and partisan battles and instead interact with others in a way that will consistently reveal the heart of God to a hurting world.

In our painfully polarized culture, we who call ourselves followers of Christ can once again be known by our love.

But how? In what context and through what means? How can we tear down the walls that divide our neighborhoods, workplaces, and families in this increasingly contentious world?

Drawing on a rich variety of true stories and sources both historical and contemporary — from behind the scenes in today's halls of power, to moving accounts from church history, to powerful breakthroughs in Jim Daly's own life and ministry — *Refocus* challenges us to reclaim our responsibility, and our privilege, as God's sons and daughters.

With the humility and compassion of Jesus as our model, *ReFocus* demonstrates how Christians can show the world an inexplicable taste of grace with no agenda other than to reveal the heart of God as the loving *Abba* Father he is.

Available in stores and online!

The Family project™
A Divine Reflection